I

CHARLIE FOXTROT

To shed light on today's cultural, social, economic, and political issues that are shaping our future as Canadians, Dundurn's **Point of View** books offer readers the informed opinions of knowledgeable individuals.

The author of a **Point of View** book is someone we've invited to address a vital topic because his or her front-line experience, arising from personal immersion in the issue, gives readers an engaging perspective, even though a reader may not ultimately reach all the same conclusions as the author.

Our publishing house is committed to framing the hard choices facing Canadians in a way that will spur democratic debate in our country. For over forty years, Dundurn has been "defining Canada for Canadians." Now our **Point of View** books, under the direction of general editor J. Patrick Boyer, take us a further step on this journey of national discovery.

Authors of **Point of View** books have an important message, and a definite point of view about an issue close to their hearts. Some **Point of View** books resemble manifestos for action, others shed light on a crucial subject from an alternative perspective, and a few are concise statements of a timely case needing to be clearly made.

But whatever the topic or whomever the author, all these titles are eye-openers for Canadians, engaging issues that matter to us as citizens.

J. Kirk Howard
President

A Note from the General Editor

Over early morning pre-conference coffee, Kim Richard Nossal and I were catching up with one another before taking our place as speakers on Canadian policy in historical context, and quickly found ourselves talking about the military procurement fiasco then enveloping the Harper government in its final days.

I'd long cherished the optimistic realism that invests Professor Nossal's political analysis and his masterly domination of subjects on which he focuses. My years in the House of Commons with the Mulroney government as parliamentary secretary, first for external affairs and then for national defence, and my role in Pugwash dealing with nuclear weapons and disarmament, further heightened my respect for his informed views about our inchoate inability as a nation to act with decisive purpose on most public issues. I'd seen first-hand how governments win buy-in for a program by overpromising its benefits and understating its costs. This is a Canadian norm, but when it concerns defence procurement, the practice is ruinous because the costs are dramatically higher.

In *Charlie Foxtrot*, Nossal unravels why. From details of military hardware to the swamp of long-brewing controversies, over the hurdles of bureaucratic process, and around the intense partisanship that scorches public debate over Canada's military roles and what equipment is needed to fulfill them, Nossal renders a true national service in clarifying for Canadians the deep-seated political problems that hobble us. Just as vital, he shows what we pointedly must demand of our elected representatives, and how a more mature Canadian political culture can embrace a sane balance between rival interests as ever-changing technologies impose the need to evolve the equipment of our armed forces in phase with the times.

J. Patrick Boyer
General Editor
Point of View Books

CHARLIE FOXTROT

Other Point of View Titles

Off the Street
by W.A. Bogart
Foreword by Sukanya Pillay

Two Freedoms
by Hugh Segal
Foreword by Tom Axworthy

Irresponsible Government
by Brent Rathgeber
Foreword by Andrew Coyne

Time Bomb
by Douglas L. Bland
Foreword by Bonnie Butlin

CHARLIE FOXTROT

Fixing Defence Procurement in Canada

KIM RICHARD NOSSAL

Foreword by Ferry de Kerckhove

DUNDURN
A J. PATRICK BOYER BOOK
TORONTO

Printer: Webcom

Library and Archives Canada Cataloguing in Publication

Nossal, Kim Richard, author
      Charlie foxtrot : fixing defence procurement in Canada / Kim Richard Nossal ; foreword by Ferry de Kerckhove.

(Point of view)
Includes bibliographical references.
Issued in print and electronic formats.
ISBN 978-1-4597-3675-7 (paperback).--ISBN 978-1-4597-3676-4 (pdf).--
ISBN 978-1-4597-3677-1 (epub)

1. Canada. Canadian Armed Forces--Procurement. 2. Canada--Armed Forces--Procurement. 3. Canada. Canadian Armed Forces--Appropriations and expenditures. 4. Canada--Armed Forces--Appropriations and expenditures. 5. Canada--Armed Forces--Finance. I. Title. II. Series: Point of view (Dundurn Press)

UC265.C3N67 2016   355.6'2120971   C2016-905421-7
                                                 C2016-905422-5

1   2   3   4   5   20   19   18   17   16

We acknowledge the support of the **Canada Council for the Arts** and the **Ontario Arts Council** for our publishing program. We also acknowledge the financial support of the **Government of Ontario**, through the **Ontario Book Publishing Tax Credit** and the **Ontario Media Development Corporation**, and the **Government of Canada**.

VISIT US AT

Dundurn
3 Church Street, Suite 500
Toronto, Ontario, Canada
M5E 1M2

For Colin and Rowan

CONTENTS

FOREWORD

I t was with a great sense of honour coupled with humility that I accepted the invitation to write a foreword to this gem of a book on Canada's defence procurement history. Indeed, I have read *Charlie Foxtrot* as a citizen, former executive vice president of the Conference of Defence Associations Institute (CDAI), and the author or co-author of four editions of CDAI's yearly *The Strategic Outlook for Canada.*[1] As a citizen, the very thorough reminder that so many lives have been lost and so much treasure wasted due to ill-conceived policies and unwarranted political gamesmanship is deeply disheartening. As a researcher who has written extensively on foreign affairs, defence policy, and national security, there is so much I agree with Kim Nossal's analysis that I could easily stop here....

But this book superbly links a set of observations at the heart of several of our greatest weaknesses as a nation on defence — champagne tastes with beer allocation; easy riders and penny pinchers, yet demanding a combat-capable, multi-role, fully equipped military; putting economic benefits ahead of military efficiency, political expediency ahead of long-term interests; and then some. One can add to the list: often ignoring our geography or twisting it — quite a big chunk — to justify doing less, putting our very sovereignty at risk, using our three oceans and the longest coastline in the world not as an inducement to develop a real national security strategy based on a clear-eyed foreign policy, but as a reason to stall fundamental decisions. Also, an apparent passion for the mythic attraction of the Great North and even of the need to defend it against those "terrible" Russians and their antiquated strategic Bear bombers, but with a minimal capability on the ground. Erich Maria Remarque has never been less alone in his *All Quiet on the Western Front*. But as Wests go, our West is bound to become less quiet, Ottawa East notwithstanding.

In a way, Nossal's book, a beautiful standalone piece, is also a synthesis — a capsule of how Canadians, who, in times of war, from Vimy onward have been recognized as top soldiers, seem to fall in a collective amnesia once the engagement ends — no more evident than the morning after the last men and women in uniform returned from Afghanistan. It is this kind of amnesia that allows our governments — unwittingly or not — to put national defence as just one of the issues on the agenda to be dealt with along the others. I am not pleading for uniqueness — each governing agenda item is unique — but defence, particularly defence procurement which is at its foundation, simply does not fit a yearly time horizon or happenstance attention. In fact, one could argue that, provided continuous due diligence is enforced, defence procurement should not be clogged into fiscal year frameworks, which is the most important reason for procurement funds unspent, with its companion impact on yearly inflation cost at 7.5 percent.[2] The irony is that the financial cycle is a yearly one, although procurement decisions usually impact future governments still to be elected. Considering that, ultimately, defence involves flesh and blood, how can Canadians accept their governments entertaining constant, systemic procurement messes? Do we forget that those men and women who join the Canadian forces agree to sacrifice their lives if needed in order to protect our nation, or participate in expeditionary missions in faraway places for the better good of humanity?

What makes Nossal's contribution so important is its exquisite fairness in analyzing such a difficult issue as procurement. Indeed, notwithstanding the huge amounts involved, the most critical issue remains to what extent the equipment procured will ensure the effectiveness of the mission and the safety of our soldiers. Simple as that. And as an observer of the CF-18 replacement saga, I wish, from the outset, to express my gratitude to Nossal for underlining General Paul Manson's outstanding contribution to the earlier, almost perfect management of the New Fighter Aircraft Program that brought us the CF-18. I, too, have benefitted from Paul's wise counsel, always offered with the modest authority of intelligence and experience.

It is with certain nostalgia that I read Professor Nossal's description of the CF-105 Arrow, which begins with a reference to Canadians' mythological memory of the aircraft. In my youth in Belgium, a comic strip in the weekly *Tintin* magazine had a Canadian pilot, Dan Cooper, flying the Arrow — which, by the way, could take-off vertically, trumping the Harrier "jump jet."

The myth endured and I made it mine when I came to Canada in 1966. The Iltis Jeep deal was the talk of the town in Brussels when I was at NATO in the early 1980s. It is extraordinarily sad that a few years later the refusal to call the operation in Afghanistan a "counter-insurgency war" and to provide the right equipment to wage it, as opposed to calling it a "peace-support mission," would lead to so many deaths, including that of my former number two in Pakistan, Glyn Berry.

Despite various studies, recommendations, tinkering, unending consultations, and brilliant ideas, the Canadian defence procurement process is and remains in deep trouble. Are we the worst within NATO? One could surmise from earlier statements by U.S. Defense Secretary Chuck Hagel that the Pentagon is even in worse shape. In fact, there is hardly a single defence department that is not hitting some kind of bow wave, with most essential decisions being punted away on the lap of future governments. It is a fact of life that defence is systematically the prime candidate for deficit reduction measures, cloaked under hypocritical terminology such as "Defence Renewal." Worse, in a way, the *Canada First Defence Strategy* of 2008 — basically a shopping list — was underfunded *ab initio*. It doesn't seem to matter which government is in power — it always succeeds to make a mess of things. Having our rock-star prime minister declare in the House of Commons that the most advanced fighter aircraft in the world, a few months away from being declared "IOC" (initial operational capability), "does not work" exemplifies the general unease with the procurement file. On the F-35 vs. Super Hornet present debate, although I have written elsewhere that the F-35 is most likely the best fighter aircraft in the world at present, that does not necessarily mean that the government should buy it, but it will certainly need to explain why and account for it, rather than simply writing it off.[3]

This is why Nossal's policy prescriptions deserve careful attention. Although I do agree with him that the politics of procurement, in its vile form, should be eradicated, a strong case can be made for at least reducing the failings of the system at the structural level through, for instance, the creation of a professional civilian-military procurement organization. The latter would be staffed with professionals having benefitted from specific training and education in procurement and making it a full career, thus avoiding the competence shortfalls made worse by the boom and bust approach to equipment purchases, a point ably made many times by my old friend and co-author George Petrolekas. Continuity and retention of knowledge are essential. Key allies have established separate acquisition agencies. Vice-Admiral Mark Norman once said aptly: "We know ships and what they need but we are no experts in procurement." But at the end of the day "it is politics, stupid," and Kim Nossal is absolutely right: a change in our political culture on these matters is a necessary condition for progress — but is it sufficient? Let the readers of this excellent book judge!

Ferry de Kerckhove *is a former member of the Canadian foreign service who was high commissioner to Pakistan (1998–2001), and ambassador to Indonesia (2001–03) and Egypt (2008–11). At present he is a senior fellow at the Graduate School of Public and International Affairs at the University of Ottawa, fellow of the Canadian Global Affairs Institute, and a member of the board of the Conference of Defence Associations Institute.*

INTRODUCTION

New governments in Ottawa often find that they have to fix defence procurement problems left behind by their predecessors. When the Conservatives under Stephen Harper came to office in February 2006, they inherited a number of severe procurement problems created by the Liberal governments that had been in power since 1993. But the Harper Conservatives proved unable to resolve these problems in their nine years in power. Indeed, by the time they were swept from office by the Liberals under Justin Trudeau in 2015, the Conservatives had added defence procurement messes of their own for the new Liberal government to deal with: an aging fleet of fighter jets that had been acquired by Trudeau's father, Pierre Elliott Trudeau, when he had been Liberal prime minister in the 1970s; a navy that had been largely left to rust out; and a recapitalization bill that climbed by millions of dollars each day as crucial decisions were delayed. The new prime minister immediately set about to fix the problems: he set up a special cabinet committee on defence procurement and charged his minister of national defence, Harjit Sajjan, with the task of launching a review of Canadian defence policy.

Within six months of taking office, however, the Trudeau Liberals had plunged themselves into a major defence procurement mess of their own making. Without waiting for the defence review to report, the government decided to press ahead and replace Canada's aging CF-18 Hornets. During the 2015 election campaign, Justin Trudeau had promised that a Liberal government would run an open competition for the CF-18 replacement, but that it would not allow the Lockheed Martin F-35 Lightning Joint Strike Fighter, which had been selected by the Conservatives in 2010 as the replacement for the CF-18, to compete. Once in power, Trudeau moved to implement his promise. Because his campaign promise to exclude the F-35 would actually have been illegal under Canadian law and would have exposed the government to a massive lawsuit by Lockheed Martin, the Trudeau government decided to finesse the issue by dispensing with an open competition. In July 2016, the government declared that the CF-18s had to be replaced immediately, and floated the idea of a sole source acquisition of a less capable fighter, the Boeing F/A-18E Super Hornet. Within two weeks, however, the Trudeau government tacked again: it walked back its Super Hornet idea, and instead opened a new round of consultations on the CF-18 replacement.

There were a variety of solid reasons for the Conservative choice of the F-35 in 2010. The F-35 was the most advanced fighter available to allies of the United States. It was the only fighter aircraft that the U.S. armed forces were going to be flying in the 2020s and 2030s (the result of an American decision in the 1990s to fly only one kind of fighter aircraft in the twenty-first century), and the Royal Canadian Air Force (RCAF) has always sought to ensure that its fighter fleet was fully interoperable with the U.S. Air Force (USAF). The F-35 was being developed by an international consortium of nine allied countries, and Canadian aerospace firms would be part of Lockheed Martin's global value chains when the aircraft went into production. However, while its decision to choose the F-35 was sound, the Conservative government completely botched the F-35 acquisition by "resetting" the CF-18 replacement program in 2012.

If the Trudeau government does not buy the F-35, Canadians will face huge military and financial consequences in the medium and long term. The RCAF will no longer be flying the same fighters as the USAF, and the Americans will not want less capable aircraft deployed in North American air defence alongside their F-35s against new generations of hostile aircraft. Canadian firms will be frozen out of Lockheed Martin's global supply chains. And even if a future government in Ottawa were to decide to acquire F-35s, the cost to Canadians would be huge, since two fleets of fighters cost far more to operate and maintain than a single fleet. Moreover, it is not at all clear that Canadian firms would be reinserted in the F-35's global value chains. In a stroke, therefore, the Trudeau Liberals not only exacerbated the mess that the Harper Conservatives had made of the fighter replacement, but if they do not choose the F-35 they will leave a huge mess for whatever government is in power in the early 2020s to grapple with.

The persistent recurrence of defence procurement problems — and the speed with which the Trudeau government created yet another defence procurement mess — underscores a sad reality: defence procurement is not something that Canadians do well. Indeed, there is an extraordinary consensus among those who know about defence procurement in Canada — government officials who are able to talk on the record, former bureaucrats, industry officials, academics, and media commentators — that the process for acquiring equipment for the Canadian Armed Forces (CAF) is beset with serious problems.

Those who are closest to the process are invariably critical, no doubt because they know first-hand how the system really works. The Conference of Defence Associations Institute (CDAI) and the Macdonald-Laurier Institute interviewed fifty retired and currently serving acquisition officials, political staff, consultants, and members of the defence industry; these insiders pointed to persistent problems with delays in the procurement process and the huge waste of taxpayer dollars that resulted.[1] Kevin Page, the parliamentary budget officer (PBO) between 2008 and 2013, openly characterized defence procurement in Canada as "completely broken."[2] Such a view has been echoed by senior bureaucrats who, in retirement, are freer to speak their minds than their colleagues still serving in the system. Dan Ross, who oversaw defence acquisitions as assistant deputy minister (materiel) in the Department of National Defence (DND) from 2005 until his retirement in January 2013, also used the word "broken" to characterize the procurement process, noting that he spent the last two years in his position "watch[ing] this system almost come to a dead stop."[3] Indeed, no less an authority than the current minister of national defence, Harjit Sajjan, who served two tours of duty with the CAF in Afghanistan before his election in 2015, admitted to the House of Commons Standing Committee on National Defence in March 2016 that "our procurement process has not served us, the Canadian Armed Forces, well."[4]

Those who work in the global defence industry are often willing to be critical of the Canadian defence procurement system, but because they want to sell their wares to the Canadian government, they tend to express their criticisms in private. Christyn Cianfarani, president of the defence industry's peak association — the Canadian Association of Defence and Security Industries (CADSI) — is understandably not overtly critical of the procurement process, but the long list of improvements that she believes needs to be made in the system suggests that CADSI members are not happy.[5] And, on occasion, industry's frustration with the system spills out, as it did in March 2016, when Alex Vicefield, the CEO of the Monaco-based group of companies that owns Davie, a shipbuilding yard in Lauzon, Quebec, claimed that defence procurement in Canada was "bizarre" and that Canadian naval procurement in particular was an "international embarrassment."[6]

While they may have less "inside" knowledge, those who study defence procurement are not impressed. David Perry, one of the most knowledgeable analysts of defence procurement in Canada, has described the system as "ramshackle." Michael Byers, a Canada Research Chair at the University of British Columbia, has opined that Canada's defence procurement process "is straight out of Monty Python." Others might be more measured but are no less critical. Elinor Sloan of Carleton University begins her examination of acquisition projects by noting that, "For years, successive Canadian governments have been overpromising and under-delivering on defence procurement," while her colleague Craig Stone at the Canadian Forces College argues that the system is basically "flawed." Aude-Emmanuelle Fleurant and Yannick Quéau, until recently with the Observatoire de l'économie politique de défense at Université du Québec à Montréal, have argued that the Canadian defence procurement system is characterized by "une vision parcellaire et des objectifs imprécis" (a fragmented vision and imprecise goals).[7]

The media in Canada is particularly important in helping frame — and maintain — the negative view of the procurement process. Jeffrey Simpson, the *Globe and Mail*'s national affairs columnist from 1984 to 2016, wrote in 2014 that "repeated procurement failures" have been a persistent problem, while his counterpart at the *National Post*, Andrew Coyne, has called defence procurement in Canada an "enduring fiasco." In *l'Actualité*, Alec Castonguay characterized the failed F-35 fighter jet procurement as "un processus d'acquisition bâclé" (a botched acquisition process). Scott Gilmore, a former Canadian diplomat and a *Maclean's* columnist, has called the defence procurement system a "national disgrace," making little effort to conceal his anger at the deaths of CAF members caused by procurement failures: "It is difficult to say this with sufficient emphasis without resorting to all-caps: those politicians, this government, the senior officers and the procurement bureaucrats in Ottawa deserve nothing but our contempt for the way they have managed Canada's military purchasing."[8]

The negative views of columnists are reflected more generally: whenever the media covers defence procurement, they inevitably use a set of stock phrases: fiasco, debacle, incompetence, mess, scandal, and shambles in English; *fiasco, gâchis* (mess), *gouffre financier* ("money pit"), *incompétence,* and *scandale* in French. Indeed, were the media in Canada less inhibited — or more like Jon Stewart during his *Daily Show* days — they might be tempted to use the colourful military slang for something that goes badly wrong all at once that some frustrated members of the Canadian military themselves have used to describe particular defence procurements (though military officers invariably tend to be polite and use the euphemistic military phonetic code "Charlie Foxtrot" instead).[9]

Is such a negative reputation deserved? I argue that, on balance, it is, and not only because one can find so few voices in Canada — in English or French — who are willing to claim publicly that the defence procurement system in general is working well enough that there is no need to reform it.

To be sure, even critics will readily acknowledge that getting defence acquisition "right" is one of the most difficult and complex policy tasks facing all liberal-democratic governments and that, therefore, Canada's travails are little different from the problems being experienced by friends and allies. And it is true that there tends to be a focus on failures rather than successes, particularly because some procurements have gone spectacularly wrong, such as the Sea King helicopter replacement. This procurement has achieved well-deserved infamy: as the military historian Aaron Plamondon concluded, this replacement project "could be the most poorly executed military procurement ever undertaken — anywhere."[10] And he wrote this in 2010 — before further problems with the Sea King replacement, the Sikorsky CH-148 Cyclone, emerged, as we will see in Chapter 2. Indeed, if Sikorsky actually manages to meet its commitment to deliver the final block of Cyclones in 2021, this replacement project, originally started in 1975 during the Liberal government of Pierre Elliott Trudeau, will have taken over forty-five years to complete, a record delay that puts Plamondon's "worst-ever-anywhere" ranking beyond any doubt.

While there is indeed a tendency to highlight the failures and gloss over the successes, the *overall* record of Canadian defence procurement, particularly in the last twenty-five years, has not been a happy one. The persistence and pervasiveness of delays in major defence acquisition projects have been more widespread and more commonplace. And it can be suggested that a delay in a procurement is perhaps even more corrosive than a spectacular failure, since it attracts comparatively less attention while often wasting far more money and causing far more serious degradation in Canadian military capacity.

And virtually every major procurement project — known as Transformational and Major Crown Projects[11] in Canadian government parlance — has been delayed. If we add the spectacular failures — such as the Sea King or the CF-18 replacements — to the many procurements that are experiencing long delays, it would not be inappropriate to suggest that the euphemism for the rude military slang that forms the title of this book* is indeed well-deserved. While there have been some successes, they do not cancel out the many messes that litter the landscape of defence procurement in Canada.

---

* It is not by coincidence that the book's title can also refer to the organization most negatively affected by the dysfunctional defence procurement system, the Canadian Forces (CF). However, I prefer to use the other official name of Canada's military, the Canadian Armed Forces (CAF), since it more accurately reflects the purpose and the essence of this institution. The two official names are the result of the purposeful ambiguity of the National Defence Act, 1985, which allows Canadians, if they wish, to strip the armed essence from the military's name. Sec. 14 reads: "The Canadian Forces are the armed forces of Her Majesty raised by Canada and consist of one Service called the Canadian Armed Forces." Prior to 2006, Canadian politicians routinely used CF when they referred to the military; indeed, even the military referred to itself in this way. When the Conservatives under Stephen Harper came to power in February 2006, they began using the other name, Canadian Armed Forces, a practice continued by the Liberal government of Justin Trudeau.

PLAN OF THE BOOK

This book has three basic purposes. First, it seeks to survey the defence procurement landscape and show how governments, both Liberal and Conservative, have managed the complexities of defence procurement so poorly that hundreds of millions of dollars have been routinely wasted, and, just as importantly, Canada and the Canadian Armed Forces have been deprived of much-needed military capacity. Second, it seeks to explain *why* we see what we do — in other words, why the system is so dysfunctional. Finally, it offers a set of suggestions for "fixing" how Canada acquires equipment for the armed forces, so that this dysfunctional and wasteful system can be improved in the years ahead.

I begin by looking at the landscape of Canadian defence procurement. The purpose here is not to provide a detailed history. Rather, I look at procurement by telling six stories. Four are historical: the Ross rifle, which was the standard issue weapon for Canadian troops at the beginning of the First World War; the CF-105 Arrow jet fighter; and the Iltis jeeps and the *Victoria*-class submarines, both of which were acquired by the government of Jean Chrétien in the late 1990s. And in the following chapter, I survey two ongoing procurements that have not gone well: the process of replacing the Sea King helicopters and the CF-18 fighters.

The six stories in these two chapters are designed to provide a backdrop for a more general conclusion about the state of procurement in Canada. While some readers may wonder what relevance stories from the distant past have today, I argue that these cases are important because historical patterns inexorably impress themselves on contemporary national policymaking, even if only in inchoate ways. For example, there is an important link between the Canadian soldiers who were sent to France to fight in the First World War in early 1915 with rifles that jammed in the mud of the trenches of the Western Front and the Canadians who were sent to Afghanistan in 2003 with soft-skinned vehicles that afforded soldiers no protection against improvised explosive devices (IEDs) and suicide bombers. And that link is a failure of the defence procurement system in Canada to get it right.

The past is important for another reason: what happens in the past invariably has an impact on the future, for these decisions set in motion a heavily path-dependent sequence of events. Consider the long-term impact of the efforts by the Canadian government to develop an indigenous fighter industry in the 1950s. The failure of the CF-105 Arrow — and its formal cancellation by the Progressive Conservative government of John Diefenbaker in February 1959 — cast long shadows in defence procurement that resonate today when Canada is re-equipping the RCAF with a new generation of fighters.

I then turn to an explanation of the trends we see in military acquisition — in other words, why the system functions (or doesn't, as the case may be) as it does. Because of the highly contested and highly political nature of defence procurement in Canada, there is little agreement on what "causes" the dysfunction that virtually all who look at defence procurement claim is its key characteristic. Yet getting the explanation right is, of course, crucial, for how one explains the defence procurement mess will determine what kinds of prescriptions are offered to improve the system.

Looking at both failures and successes, I revisit some of the standard explanations for who is actually responsible for the mess that is defence procurement in Canada, and I suggest that much of the blame is in fact misdirected. I argue that, while it is fashionable to lay the responsibility for the dysfunctions at the bureaucratic level — where the actual process of defence procurement unfolds — in fact we have to look elsewhere to understand why Canadians have been so ill-served and why governments have found it so difficult to equip the CAF efficiently.

In particular, I conclude that we must look at the *principals* in the process, not their *agents* — in other words, ministers in cabinet (and would-be ministers in the Official Opposition), and not civil servants in the bureaucracy or officers in the military. I conclude that it is the elected representatives in the two major parties — the Liberals and the Conservatives — who are primarily responsible for the dysfunctions we see in defence procurement in Canada. For, as I will show, both of the major parties, in and out of power, have not been willing to grasp the nettle and try and reconcile the contradictions of defence policy in Canada.

FIXING THE "MESS"

I then turn to what is the most important purpose of this book: how we might do better in the future. Although the media often uses the word "mess" to describe defence procurement in Canada, they tend to mean it in its colloquial sense: "an untidy or jumbled or confused state of affairs." By contrast, I frame the procurement system in Canada as a mess in the social science sense: a "system of problems that produces dissatisfaction," to use Russell L. Ackoff's well-known definition. These problems, Ackoff suggested, are independent of each other, "but with dynamic situations that consist of complex systems of changing problems that interact with each other."[12] Unlike "wicked problems" in public policy — policy problems that are so difficult and intractable that they defy solution[13] — public policy "messes" are resolvable precisely because the resolution is not intractable. By contrast, each of the systems in the interactive "system of problems" can in fact be addressed and thus could, in theory at least, be resolved. That is why Ackoff argues that what is needed is "mess management": ways of resolving problems within each of the various systems — and subsystems — that together comprise defence procurement in Canada.

These systems are numerous.[14] Defence procurement involves the interaction of elected officials, their political staff, civil servants, and actors from both private industry and the not-for-profit sector, particularly former members of the armed forces. The systems of interactions between these actors are framed within formal legal, legislative, regulatory, and budgetary frameworks, each operating separately but interdependently. These actors operate in a marketplace of sorts, but one that is unique in its shape and operation. Military requirements and the capabilities of military equipment itself comprise systems in themselves, as do the various stages in weapons system development — concept and technology development, system development and demonstration, production and deployment, and sustainment and disposal (as these stages are called by the U.S. Department of Defense). The various stages in the procurement process — calling for proposals, evaluating responses, selecting winners, signing contracts, taking deliveries, and training operators — are systems. There are also systems needed to maintain equipment that is purchased over long service lives, and yet other systems needed to extend the service lives of military equipment. In short, there are many systems that can develop (and in the Canadian context have developed) the "system of problems" requiring "mess management."

However, fixing the procurement mess and getting defence procurement right has remained frustratingly elusive. It certainly is not for want of prescriptions, particularly from those who have worked in different parts of the procurement system itself. As we will see in Chapter 4, many of those who know the defence procurement process best tend to focus on organizational or procedural fixes — reshaping the *process* by which defence equipment is procured. Thus, for example, a favourite "fix" is to abandon the shared authority model, under which the minister of national defence, the minister of public services and procurement, and the minister of innovation, science, and economic development are collectively responsible for defence procurement. Instead, some advocate the creation of a separate agency, with its own minister in cabinet, that would alone be responsible for defence procurement. Others focus on reshaping the broader economic environment in which national defence priorities are decided. Others still focus our attention on how DND prioritizes its acquisitions.

I would not disagree that focusing on the organizational or bureaucratic or budgetary systems would improve defence procurement in Canada. However, I will argue that the ultimate cause of the present dysfunction in defence procurement is not the procurement system; rather, the messes are the result of the broader political environment in which defence procurement decisions are made. It follows that, without a change in that environment, we are not going to see a marked change in defence procurement outcomes in Canada, no matter how many organizational reforms are embraced.

Thus, the concluding chapter offers a set of *political* prescriptions for defence acquisitions: changes that politicians in both of Canada's major political parties need to make in their behaviour and their attitudes — in other words, in the *culture* — if we are going to avoid the waste, the dysfunction, and the loss of military capability that is so much a mark of the defence procurement process in Canada today. I argue that politicians — both those in cabinet and in the Official Opposition — need to be more realistic in shaping defence policy; they need to frame the tasks and missions assigned to the Canadian Armed Forces more carefully and judiciously than they have in the past. I suggest that Canadian politicians need to stop playing politics with defence procurement, since the worst dysfunctions in defence procurement in Canada have been caused by politicization. Instead, politicians, both government and Official Opposition, need to recognize that the long timelines in defence procurement mean that there is a necessary symbiosis in this area of policy: the consequences of decisions taken during one parliament will not generally be felt until much later, usually well past the next election. A more bipartisan approach to defence procurement, I conclude, would go a considerable distance to eliminating the dysfunctions we see in the present system.

This is, I acknowledge, a political scientist's fix, rather than the kind of fix that might be offered by an expert in public administration or the science of defence procurement. But the Canadian defence procurement system is a mess primarily because of politics, as we will see, and so it should be at the political level that we begin to address the problem.

1

GETTING IT WRONG: A CENTURY OF DEFENCE PROCUREMENT MESSES

Effective defence procurement, Alan Williams has written, ensures that the Canadian Armed Forces have "the right equipment, at the right time, in the right place, with the right support" — and "at the right price."[1] Williams should know whereof he speaks: for ten years he was an assistant deputy minister (ADM) who oversaw $11.2 billion in acquisitions for two departments. Recently, Canadian governments haven't always managed to get defence procurement quite "right" on any of these criteria. By 2016, every major defence procurement was in some kind of trouble — mostly as a result of delays of one kind or another.

It should be noted, though, that over the last hundred years — through two world wars; an intervention against the Bolsheviks in 1919; a police action in Korea from 1950 to 1953; armed actions against Iraq in 1991, Serbia in 1999, and Libya in 2011; a twelve-and-half-year mission in Afghanistan; and participation in the global coalition to counter the Islamic State in Iraq and the Levant (ISIL) after 2014, together with numerous peacekeeping and disaster relief missions — the Canadian government has conducted thousands of procurement programs of all sizes for the armed forces, most of them getting it more or less right on Williams's various criteria.

At the same time, however, Canadian defence acquisitions have been marked by a number of messes — as we defined that term in the introduction — that had significant impacts on the armed forces or the defence system. The purpose of this chapter is to profile four historical procurement messes as a way of demonstrating how defence procurement has consistently gone wrong. The cases are the acquisition of the Ross rifle before the First World War; the attempt to develop a Canadian fighter-interceptor, the Avro Canada CF-105 Arrow, in the 1950s; the Iltis jeep replacement in the late 1990s; and the *Victoria*-class submarine purchase, also begun in the late 1990s. Two messes — the Sea King helicopter replacement, the longest-running defence procurement in Canadian history, and the aborted F-35 fighter jet acquisition — are ongoing, and are surveyed in the next chapter.

THE ROSS RIFLE

The Ross rifle was standard equipment for Canadian troops who were sent to France after the outbreak of the First World War in August 1914.[2] It had its origins in Canada's participation in the Boer War (or, as it is officially known in Canada, the South African War) fought between 1899 and 1902. At the time, Canada had no indigenous industrial capacity in arms manufacture, and thus the government in Ottawa was entirely dependent on supplies from the Imperial government in London, which allocated weapons that were surplus to British needs to other parts of the Empire, sometimes as gifts, sometimes as purchases.

In 1900, after the Liberal government of Sir Wilfrid Laurier committed troops to the war, it needed rifles for those troops. The minister of militia, Frederick Borden, tried to place an order in Britain for ten thousand Lee-Enfield .303-inch calibre bolt-action repeating rifles, the standard rifle issued to Imperial troops, but the War Office could spare only two thousand rifles, since there were not enough Lee-Enfields in production to supply British troops. So Borden went to two British manufacturers, seeking to have the Lee-Enfield produced in Canada under licence, but neither was interested. As a result, the Laurier government began to consider manufacturing a Canadian rifle.

Borden's son Harold was killed in action at Witpoort in July 1900, adding grief to his frustrations with the British. He was thus very receptive when, in early 1901, Sir Charles Ross, a Scottish entrepreneur, approached him with a proposal to manufacture a rifle that he had invented. Ross's rifle had a "straight-pull" bolt action rather than the rotating bolt action of the Lee-Enfield, allowing faster rates of fire. Borden was sufficiently impressed that he agreed to create a committee to consider the Ross rifle and test it against the Lee-Enfield. The testing, such as it was, was not rigorous: one of Ross's friends was on the committee, and Ross himself was allowed to be present for the tests and was even observed oiling one of the test Lee-Enfields, presumably in an effort to ensure that it jammed.[3] Borden decided to ignore the one member who expressed concerns about the number of times that the Ross misfired and jammed during endurance trials, and he awarded Ross a contract that enabled him to start the Ross Rifle Company, which promised to create one thousand jobs in Laurier's riding of Quebec East.

In 1902, Ross was given a nineteen-acre factory site on land owned by the Department of Militia and Defence in the Cove Fields area of the Plains of Abraham for $1 a year. Ross was also given a lucrative contract that set the price at $25 per rifle, well above the $15 to $18 it would have cost had the Canadian government purchased Lee-Enfields from Britain. The encouragement of an infant industry that would provide Canada with an autonomous and indigenous supply of rifles, it might be noted, was very much in keeping with the other "lessons" that Borden took from his experience in 1900, including his attempts to encourage a citizen army of sharpshooters, his subsidization of rifle clubs, and his support for military training in schools.[4]

Ironically, faced with this open challenge to its monopoly on small arms, the Imperial government tried to dissuade the Canadians. Joseph Chamberlain, the colonial secretary, stressed to Ottawa "the very great importance of adhering to absolute uniformity of pattern in the weapons" used by the Empire, expressing the hope that whatever arms Canada manufactured would be "identical" to Imperial weapons, and offering to produce weapons for Canada. Borden refused; the most that he would promise London was that the Canadian rifle would use .303-inch ammunition, the same calibre as the Lee-Enfield.

In the years that followed, one of the most ardent champions of the Ross was Sam Hughes, a Conservative member of parliament and a friend of Sir Charles Ross. In 1907, Sir Frederick, as the minister of militia had become in 1902, had taken the unusual step of appointing Hughes, an opposition MP, as chair of a special Standing Small Arms Committee in the Department of Militia, in a stroke neutralizing criticism of the Ross rifle that was emerging among the Conservative opposition. In this role, Hughes became increasingly involved in the development of the Ross. A staunch and aggressive Canadian nationalist, he was deeply committed to the self-sufficiency in small arms that the Ross represented, believing that what he routinely called the "best rifle in the world" could place Canada as a leader in small-arms manufacturing.

In 1911, Hughes was appointed minister of militia and defence in the Conservative government of Sir Robert Borden (a cousin of Sir Frederick), and the Ross rifle was formally adopted as the "national arm" for the Canadian forces. As minister, Hughes played an important role in marketing the Ross, not only to Canadians, but also to other countries in the British Empire, in the hopes that the rifle would be adopted by their armed forces. Hughes was an expert marksman and a former president of the Dominion Rifle Association, and he routinely inserted himself in the production process to propose design changes to ensure that the rifle competed well in the prestigious shooting competitions organized by the National Rifle Association at Bisley, widely regarded as a testing ground for military weapons. Much to the chagrin of the Canadians, the National Rifle Association went to considerable lengths to keep the Ross rifle out of the competition between 1906 and 1908. When it was finally allowed to compete in 1909, Canadian shooters won numerous prizes.

The Ross rifle performed very well in peacetime. Its long and heavy barrel gave it exceptional accuracy and distance. At Hugh's insistence, its chamber was purposely designed around the ammunition it used — high-quality cartridges produced by Dominion Arsenal Company, the Canadian government-owned ammunition manufacturing facility in Quebec City — and the tight fit produced higher muzzle velocity. The civilian version of the rifle proved popular with hunters, and the match target version continued to do well on the competition circuit.

But, as Ronald Haycock has noted, "it never occurred to Sam Hughes that fine accuracy was not the sole requirement of a rifle in war."[5] When the troops of the Canadian Expeditionary Force arrived in France in February 1915 with their Ross rifles, many of them discovered that their weapon did not work well in battlefield conditions. The Ross was eight inches longer than the Lee-Enfield, making it more difficult to use in the trenches. The bayonet had a tendency to fall off when the rifle was fired. If the weapon was not kept scrupulously clean — almost impossible in the mud of the trenches and no-man's land — the bolt would often jam, particularly when it was fired repeatedly. And while the "straight pull" bolt mechanism could be easily disassembled for cleaning, it was easy to reassemble the bolt without the locking lugs engaged, which would damage the bolt (and sometimes injure the shooter) the next time the weapon was fired.[6]

Most importantly, the Ross proved sensitive to the quality of the ammunition being used. When it was fed the well-crafted, exact-dimension cartridges produced by the Dominion Arsenal Company, it was fine. However, Dominion Arsenal could not supply the Canadian troops with sufficient cartridges, so they had to use British-made .303 ammunition that was being mass-produced for Imperial troops on the Western Front. The British ammunition was of poorer quality: the soft brass used tended to expand in the tight Ross chamber; it was also "dirtier," with more lead and powder fouling, exacerbating the jamming problem.

In the first combat test faced by the Ross, the second battle of Ypres in April 1915, a third of the Canadian troops simply threw their rifles away. Indeed, it was after Ypres that the story that Canadian soldiers went about picking up the much sturdier Lee-Enfields from dead British soldiers began to circulate. Needless to say, the troops in the field were not happy with a weapon that was quickly nicknamed the "Canadian club." Complaints about the performance of the Ross immediately made their way up the chain of command. As one unidentified Canadian officer wrote shortly after the second battle of Ypres, "It is nothing short of murder to send out men against the enemy with such a weapon."[7] The British commander of the first Canadian contingent, Maj.-Gen. Edwin Alderson, recommended to the Imperial commander-in-chief, Sir John French, that the Ross be withdrawn from service and that Canadians be issued with Lee-Enfield rifles.

But the reaction in Ottawa to the problems being faced by Canadian troops in the field was deeply political. Since he was so personally committed to the Ross rifle, Hughes's immediate reaction was to defend it. He appointed a committee to look into the faults but thought nothing of including Sir Charles Ross as one of its members. Hughes insisted that the root of the problems lay in low-quality British ammunition and refused to abandon the Ross. Finally, in February 1916, after months of resistance by Hughes, Alderson sent all the evidence of the Ross's failure on the battlefield to Maj.-Gen. Sir Willoughby Gwatkin, the British officer who served as Canadian Chief of the General Staff. Hughes immediately launched a personal attack against Alderson, claiming to the House of Commons that the British general "did not know the butt from the muzzle" of the rifle about which he was complaining.[8]

Sir Robert Borden took Hughes's side, prompting the British Imperial high command to remove Alderson from his Canadian command in May 1916 rather than challenge a dominion prime minister. However, when Alderson's evidence was leaked to the *Ottawa Citizen* and published in May, Hughes's position became increasingly untenable. Borden agreed to withdraw the Ross and have Canadian troops armed with Lee-Enfields. Hughes was further sidelined when the prime minister created a new cabinet position to coordinate and administer the Canadian Expeditionary Force and appointed Sir George Perley, the Canadian high commissioner in London, as minister of overseas forces in October 1916. This prompted an extraordinary exchange of letters between Hughes and the prime minister in which Hughes accused Borden of lying, prompting the prime minister to demand Hughes's resignation.[9]

With its principal defender gone, "that damned Ross rifle," as so many Canadians and British were wont to describe it,[10] was done as Canada's "national arm." The Ross Rifle Company was expropriated by the government in 1917, production of the rifles was brought to an end, and the factory's buildings in Cove Fields put to other uses before being demolished in 1931 to make way for an underground reservoir to supply Quebec City with water.

THE CF-105 ARROW

The Avro Canada CF-105 Arrow remains the most iconic example of a Canadian defence procurement project gone wrong, though most Canadians have an entirely mythological memory of the Arrow.[11] In the 1950s, the Canadian government tried to have fighter aircraft acquired for the RCAF built in Canada. The main fighter, the CF-100 "Canuck," a long-range interceptor, was Canadian-designed and produced by Avro Canada, a subsidiary of A.V. Roe and Company, a British aircraft company. However, the CF-100 was a subsonic fighter, and the development of supersonic bombers had made it obsolete. As a result, the Liberal government of Louis St. Laurent approved a replacement program for the CF-100 in December 1953, with the expectation that a new supersonic fighter would be in service by 1958.

Clearly attracted by the idea that Canada could become a leading manufacturer of high-end fighter aircraft, the St. Laurent government committed to producing a fighter-interceptor that, if produced, would be a world-class interceptor. The RCAF had outlined specifications that placed it far ahead of other aircraft in development at the time. It had to have a supersonic combat radius of two hundred nautical miles; it had to be able to climb to a ceiling of sixty thousand feet, with a climb rate of fifty thousand feet in six minutes; and it had to have all-weather capability. The aircraft had to have two engines because of Canadian geography — its huge and largely uninhabited landmass required extended range — but also to provide protection for the aircrew in the event of engine failure. Moreover, because Canada lacked the advanced ground-based navigational infrastructure of the continental United States, the RCAF also argued that a Canadian interceptor needed a navigator.

No other foreign-made fighter could meet the RCAF requirements, so in 1955 the St. Laurent government formally decided to develop a Canadian plane. The delta-winged CF-105 Arrow, proposed by Avro Canada, was capable of all-weather operation, speeds of close to Mach-2, and altitudes of fifty thousand feet. The original plans in the early 1950s had called for a fleet of five hundred to six hundred aircraft for the RCAF, though this was eventually reduced to four hundred.

Although it was a Canadian fighter, the original plans called for only one component to be developed and built in Canada: the airframe. The other major components — the engine, fire-control system, and weapons system — would be developed and sourced offshore. But, one by one, these other components would become a Canadian responsibility. The engine initially chosen was the Wright J-67, a British turbojet engine produced under licence by Wright Aeronautical Corporation for the Convair F-102 delta-winged interceptor being developed for the USAF. Unfortunately for Avro, Wright fell behind in its development schedule, and in 1955 the USAF abandoned the J-67 and turned to another engine. So Avro proposed an engine that was being developed by another A.V. Roe subsidiary in Canada, Orenda Engines, and the Canadian government agreed to fund the development of the Orenda PS-13 Iroquois engine as well as the airframe.

For the CF-105's fire-control system, the RCAF wanted a forty-inch radar disk, much larger than the disks then in use in USAF fighters. The leading manufacturer of aircraft radar disks, Hughes Aircraft Company in the United States, was not willing to develop a larger disk for Canada's small production run. So Canada took responsibility for the development of the radar, which was contracted to RCA-Victor in New Jersey. But RCA had much less experience, and their ASTRA system proved to be increasingly expensive and encountered a number of delays in development.

Finally, Canada also assumed responsibility for the air-to-air missile used by the CF-105. The original plans called for a Canadian-designed missile built by Canadair, the "Velvet Glove." But changes in technology meant that by 1955 this missile was no longer adequate. So rather than spend more money upgrading it, the government decided to purchase the licence rights to the Sparrow II, an American air-to-air missile being developed for the U.S. Navy (USN) by Douglas Aircraft Company. However, in 1956 the USN abandoned the Sparrow II when it was in the final stages of development. Canada was offered Sparrow Is or IIIs instead, but the government decided to finish developing the Sparrow II in Canada at a facility in Hamilton, Ontario. All three of these systems subsequently experienced delays in development, incurring additional expenses.

At the very time that the costs of the CF-105 were climbing because of the addition of these indigenously developed systems, the RCAF reduced its requirement for the number of aircraft it needed. Originally, there were to be four hundred aircraft, with nine regular squadrons and eleven squadrons for the reserves. However, as the aircraft's development evolved, the RCAF was discovering that auxiliary pilots were having difficulty getting the training time necessary to fly the CF-100s; it was clear that they would never be able to get the training necessary to handle such a sophisticated aircraft as the CF-105. So the RCAF dropped the idea that the CF-105 would be flown by reserve squadrons. This dropped the number of aircraft precipitously, to just one hundred.

The delays, the additional developmental costs, and the dramatic decrease in the number of aircraft being produced all had an impact on the price of the aircraft. When the CF-105 was in prototype, in the early 1950s, the unit cost of the CF-105 was estimated at $1.5 million. By the mid-1950s, the costs had risen to between $4 million and $6 million per plane.

But neither the St. Laurent government nor the Progressive Conservative government of John Diefenbaker, which came to power after the Liberals were defeated in the June 1957 elections, was willing to try to grapple with the quickly mounting costs of the CF-105. For its part, the Liberal government was planning to cancel the program because it had grown so costly, but it was putting off the actual decision before the 1957 election, on the grounds that it would be seized on by the opposition as a campaign issue. And when the Progressive Conservative government assumed office with a minority, it too had good political reasons to punt the issue: Diefenbaker was planning to call another election as soon as practical and did not want to have to deal with what was clearly a problem. So his government quickly agreed to continue funding the project for the short term. It was only after the Progressive Conservatives won a massive majority in the general election of March 31, 1958, that the Diefenbaker government moved to address the issue of the Arrow.

By September 1958, the unit cost of the one hundred Arrows had risen to $12.5 million, and the only way that the government could consider continuing the program was if the aircraft could be exported in large numbers to bring the unit cost down. Since the start of the program, both the Liberal and Conservative governments had tried to interest both the Royal Air Force in the United Kingdom and the U.S. Air Force to agree to purchase the CF-105 as a way of reducing the cost of the aircraft. But neither the British nor the Americans were interested in acquiring the CF-105, not only because they did not need the particular Canadian requirements, but also because they had their own aircraft manufacturers that they were more interested in supporting.

It is true that in January 1958, the U.S. Secretary of the Air Force, James Douglas, offered to have the USAF purchase several squadrons of CF-105s and give them back to the RCAF for use in the new North American Air Defence (NORAD) command that had just been established. But Canada's ambassador in Washington, Norman Robertson, rejected this offer on the grounds that such "aid" from the U.S. would be "politically unacceptable" in Canada. However, as Russell Isinger notes, there was another more compelling reason: even if the USAF purchased several squadrons of CF-105s, the production run would still be too small to make the project viable.

So, in a series of meetings in February 1959, the Diefenbaker cabinet did what the Liberals would have done had they won the 1957 election: it agreed to cancel the entire Arrow program, formally announcing the cancellation on February 20. Cabinet minutes reveal that Diefenbaker himself wanted to save the CF-105 program, but he deferred to both the minister of national defence and the minister of finance, both of whom agreed with the broad consensus in the senior bureaucracy that the mounting costs of the CF-105 far outweighed the benefits. Avro immediately fired fourteen thousand employees; a further fifteen thousand employees in Avro's value chains of 650 subcontractors were affected. The Conservative government bought a fleet of Macdonnell CF-101 Voodoos that had been manufactured for the USAF; these fighters served as Canada's interceptors until the early 1980s, when they were replaced by the CF-18 Hornets.

THE ILTIS JEEP

A century after the South African War, Canada was again at war, this time in Afghanistan, in an operation led by the U.S. and the North Atlantic Treaty Organization (NATO) and approved by the United Nations Security Council. Although the Canadian engagement in Afghanistan was never called a "war" by the Liberal government of Jean Chrétien that sent troops to serve in Afghanistan,[12] the reality on the ground for those members of the Canadian Armed Forces who were deployed in that country was that they were in a state of war. Their adversaries were the many individuals and groups in Afghanistan who were seeking to kill or maim those foreigners who had assisted in the ouster of the Taliban regime and had established a new government under the presidency of Hamid Karzai. Canadians in Afghanistan — troops, civilian government officials, and even private Canadian citizens working in Afghanistan — were all targets in what was unambiguously a war zone. Canadians, and other "internationals," were all considered enemies by the Taliban, who had reorganized themselves in Pakistan and were being assisted and financed by Pakistani intelligence services,[13] and thus appropriate targets for attack by ambush, suicide bombing, improvised explosive devices (IEDs), or "vehicle-borne suicide IEDs" (VBSIEDs).

But because the Canadian government did not frame the Afghanistan mission as a *war*, the CAF was deployed to Afghanistan with equipment that was not designed for a war zone. Rather, when Canadian soldiers were deployed to Kandahar in 2002, to Kabul in 2003, and then back to Kandahar in 2005, they had a mix of unarmoured and lightly armoured vehicles that had been used in previous peace and stabilization operations.

Among the vehicles initially sent to Afghanistan was the Iltis Bombardier "jeep," a light reconnaissance vehicle originally built for the German armed forces by Volkswagen AG. In 1981, production had been transferred under licence to Bombardier Inc. in Montreal, and several thousand jeeps were produced for the Canadian and Belgian armed forces, albeit at a premium price in order to generate employment in Montreal. Volkswagen AG produced the Iltis for $26,500; the Iltis Bombardier cost $84,000 each. A staple of Canada's blue-helmet past, the Iltis was soft-skinned: its doors and roof were made of canvas, and all that protected its "tub," or crew compartment, was a sheet metal bottom.

In 2002, a Canadian battle group from the 3rd battalion of Princess Patricia's Canadian Light Infantry (3 PPCLI) and the Lord Strathcona's Horse (Royal Canadians) deployed to Kandahar as part of a U.S. Brigade Combat Team. While Iltis vehicles were shipped with the Canadian forces, Col. Francis J. (Frank) Wiercinski, the U.S. commander of the combat team, refused to allow Canadian troops to patrol "outside the wire" in their Iltis jeeps; patrols were conducted using U.S. armoured Humvees.[14] However, when Canada provided forces for a peace-support mission in Kabul between 2003 and 2005, there was no such restriction. Because Operation Athena, as it was called by the Canadian Armed Forces, was seen as a peace-support mission, the forces were equipped for the kind of missions that the CAF had been engaged in for decades. Thus patrols were frequently conducted in the fleet of seventy-four Iltis jeeps that had been shipped to Afghanistan.

On October 2, 2003, an Iltis on patrol in the Jowz Valley west of Kabul hit an anti-tank mine. Two soldiers riding in the vehicle, Sgt. Robert Short and Cpl. Robbie Beerenfenger, were killed instantly; the driver, Cpl. Thomas Stirling, suffered severe burns and other injuries; two of the three soldiers travelling in an Iltis twenty metres behind them were also wounded. Canadian engineers had travelled the route that morning checking for bombs, but it was subsequently determined that the attack had in fact been organized by the Hizb-i-Islami Gulbuddin (HiG), an insurgent group aligned with the Taliban and al-Qaeda; HiG had paid contract killers to lay several explosive devices in the wheel rut of the track in between Canadian patrols.[15] This strike was followed by the death of another Canadian soldier, Cpl. Jamie Murphy, who was killed in January 2004 when a suicide bomber threw himself on the hood of Murphy's Iltis as it was patrolling the streets of Kabul.

The deaths of Cpl. Beerenfenger and Sgt. Short triggered considerable criticism back in Canada. When he had bid farewell to the troops heading to Afghanistan at Canadian Forces Base (CFB) Petawawa in July 2003, the minister of national defence, John McCallum, had promised to resign "if it is found that any Canadians died as the result of a lack of preparation or equipment." As he put it, "If we put people in harm's way, we have to give our people proper equipment. It is as simple as that."[16]

The opposition parties criticized McCallum in the House of Commons for knowingly putting Canadian troops in harm's way without appropriate protection. Echoing the phrase used in anger and frustration over the Ross rifle a century before, the defence critic for the Canadian Alliance, Jay Hill (CA: Prince George–Peace River), told McCallum that "the government should have given our troops … more lightly armoured vehicles so they did not have to use these damned jeeps." Hill wanted to know why the government had not considered the Humvee, the armoured vehicle used by the U.S. armed forces, as a possible replacement for the Iltis.

Stephen Harper, the leader of the Official Opposition, reminded McCallum that the Americans had warned Canada in 2002 about the Iltis and asked, "When will the government stop unnecessarily putting the lives of Canadian servicemen and servicewomen at risk?"

No doubt with his earlier promise in mind, McCallum flatly rejected the opposition criticisms that the troops were not appropriately protected, claiming that he had been assured by his officials that Canadian troops in Afghanistan were "well equipped." He also echoed a comment initially made to the press by Brig.-Gen. Andrew Leslie, commander of the Canadian forces in Kabul: the Iltis was a much better patrol vehicle for the streets of Kabul than a Humvee, since "[y]ou cannot win the hearts and minds of the Afghan people as you speed by in an armoured vehicle."

Peter MacKay (PC: Pictou–Antigonish–Guysborough), the leader of the Progressive Conservatives, and Joe Clark (PC: Calgary Centre) both criticized McCallum not only for sending Canadians into harm's way, but also for appearing to blame his officials.[17] Three weeks later, Cheryl Gallant (CA: Renfrew–Nipissing–Pembroke), whose riding included CFB Petawawa, read into the record a letter from one of her constituents who had attended Beerenfenger's and Short's funerals; she accused McCallum of knowing in advance that the Iltis was a "death trap."[18]

After this, however, a dramatic change in the political landscape in Ottawa caused the Iltis issue to drop off the political agenda. On December 7, 2003, the Conservative Party of Canada (CPC) was formally launched, the result of a merger between the Canadian Alliance and the Progressive Conservative party. The following spring, a party leadership convention elected Stephen Harper as the CPC leader on March 20, 2004. On December 12,

Paul Martin, who had been elected Liberal leader in November, formally replaced Chrétien as prime minister. In this new political environment, some of the contentious issues from the previous parliamentary session dropped away. Thus, when Cpl. Murphy was killed in January 2004, it was not even raised in the House. Indeed, in the third and final session of the 37th Parliament, the Iltis was mentioned only four times, three of them *en passant*.

The only substantive reference to the jeep came in response to a written question put by Loyola Hearn (CPC: St John's West) in May that asked what the government was planning to do with the Iltis fleet. Martin's new minister of national defence, David Pratt, assured the House that the jeep would not be used for operations in Afghanistan after the next "roto" (rotation) in August 2004.[19] And, just as the minister promised, over the summer of 2004, the Iltis was replaced with the Mercedes-Benz G-class Gelandwagen, known in the Canadian Army as a G Wagon, a light utility vehicle that could be lightly armoured.

The two boards of inquiry into the deaths of Beerenfenger, Short, and Murphy did not report until after the general election of June 28, 2004, which resulted in a minority government for the Martin Liberals. Neither inquiry faulted the Iltis. On the contrary: at a press conference in August 2004, senior officers of the CAF rejected all media criticism of the Iltis. Brig.-Gen. Christian Barabé, the chair of the Jowz valley inquiry, asserted that the Iltis was "an appropriate vehicle to use for the mission and task at hand." Likewise, Leslie, now a major-general and the assistant chief of the Land Staff (as the Canadian Army was known before 2011), weighed in to say that that "if I had to do it again — based on the vehicles that we had — I'd do it again." He repeated what he had said the previous year: while vehicles like an armoured Humvee offer more protection, they are difficult to manoeuvre in narrow streets. "You can't get to where you have to do your job — especially in places like Kabul." The Beerenfenger-Short board noted that the size and power of the anti-tank mine strike in their case would have caused major damage to a more heavily armoured vehicle.[20]

It is true that, had Canadians been using G Wagons instead of Iltis jeeps in the Jowz Valley in October 2003, the outcome would likely have not been different. It is highly unlikely that the light armour plating of the G Wagon would have saved Cpl. Beerenfenger and Sgt. Short, since the vehicle was not designed to protect against large IEDs or VBSIEDs, much less the kind of powerful anti-tank mine that had been laid in the rut of that Jowz Valley track. The relative lack of protection afforded by a G Wagon was evident when a Canadian convoy travelling the streets of Kandahar City was attacked with a VBSIED in January 2006. As the Canadian battle group was establishing itself in Kandahar and thus beginning to disrupt the patterns of local politics, including the drug trade, power brokers in Kandahar decided to send a message to the Canadians to warn them to back off. Glyn Berry, the Canadian diplomat who was serving as the political director of the Provincial Reconstruction Team (PRT) in Kandahar, was targeted for assassination.[21] On January 15, the G Wagon in which Berry was riding was attacked by a VBSIED: the force of the blast blew the vehicle across the road, peeling open the roof. Berry was killed instantly, and three Canadian soldiers in the convoy, Master Corporal Paul Franklin, Cpl. Jeffrey Bailey, and Pte. William Salikin, were severely injured.

While the G Wagon might not have protected Canadian troops against larger explosive devices, it would have afforded those on patrol slightly more protection than the completely unprotected Iltis. But in the debate about the Iltis that occurred after the deaths of Cpl. Beerenfenger and Sgt. Short in October 2003, what never emerged was the reason why the G Wagons were not deployed to Afghanistan until 2004. The Iltis was scheduled to be replaced by a more heavily armoured vehicle by 1999. Had that replacement occurred on time, another vehicle would have accompanied Canadian troops to Afghanistan in 2001. But, as David Pugliese of the *Ottawa Citizen* makes clear,[22] the reason why the Iltis was still in service in a war zone until late 2004 was because the replacement for this vehicle had been delayed for nearly five years as a result of political interference by the minister of national defence, Art Eggleton.

By the late 1980s, the Iltis had begun to rust out, and because it was no longer in production, spare parts were a problem. The Department of National Defence started a replacement program in November 1993, the very month that the Liberals under Jean Chrétien took office. However, the new government was committed to reducing both Canada's deficit and its debt, and reducing defence spending — the largest single discretionary item in the federal budget — was one of the prime methods used to achieve this goal. The Light Utility Vehicle Wheeled (LUVW) project was one of the many DND projects that were put on hold as part of the Chrétien government's deficit reduction program.

However, as the replacement was delayed, the Iltis fleet continued to deteriorate. Moreover, over the course of the 1990s, the government was deploying the CAF to peacekeeping operations that were increasingly dangerous. In the Balkans, Canadians serving as blue-helmet peacekeepers not only faced considerable danger from mines, but were routinely harassed and even shot at by fighters in that conflict.[23] In December

1993, for example, eleven Canadian peacekeepers were assault-
ed by Serb soldiers; on New Year's Day 1994, two Canadian
peacekeepers patrolling in an Iltis were wounded after being
fired at by Serbian forces; later in January, two further incidents
put Canadian lives in jeopardy.[24]

By 1996, the condition of the Iltis fleet had become sufficiently critical that DND made replacing it a priority. In
October 1997, the Treasury Board approved the resumption of
the LUVW program. The procurement would feature two fleets
of vehicles. A commercial off-the-shelf (COTS) variant would be
acquired for use in Canada, mainly by the reserve force. A fleet
of 802 "standard military pattern" (SMP) vehicles would be used
overseas. The SMP variant would have to be sufficiently armoured
that it was capable of withstanding mines with one kilogram of
explosives but could also be "up armoured" to withstand blasts of
6.5 kilograms. Importantly, the Treasury Board specified that the
SMP variant had to be "non-developmental" — in other words,
it had to be a vehicle that was in service with another army and
could be purchased off the shelf. The Treasury Board also set a
delivery deadline of 1999, which was when DND estimated that
the Iltis fleet would be "economically non-viable."

Three firms, all foreign, were interested in this project:
Land Rover of Coventry in the United Kingdom, which pro-
duced the Defender and the Wolf, both of which were in service
with the Australian Defence Force as well as the British Army;
Mercedes-Benz, which manufactured the Gelandwagen; and AM
General LLC of South Bend, Indiana, which manufactured the
High Mobility Multi-Purpose Wheeled Vehicle (HMMWV), or
Humvee. National Defence was scheduled to brief these compa-
nies on the LUVW program on July 14, 1998.

The briefing never took place. On June 15, 1998, Western Star Trucks of Kelowna, British Columbia, came forward with a proposal to build a vehicle that would be "designed and manufactured in Canada by Canadians." In 1992, Western Star had won the contract for 2,800 light support vehicles (or LSVs) for the CAF, which it built at its Kelowna plant as a joint venture with Iveco of Turin, Italy. The company now proposed submitting a bid to the LUVW program. Its vehicle, the M1044, was similar to the U.S. Humvee but would be based on the LSV.

Because the Treasury Board had stipulated that the LUVW could not be "developmental," the Western Star proposal should not have been entertained, since it was not in production and was not in service with another country's armed forces. However, on June 23, representatives from Western Star managed to secure a meeting with Eggleton on their proposed vehicle, arguing that since the M1044 was based on a vehicle that was in service with the CAF, it should qualify. Eggleton, presumably impressed by the number of jobs that would be created in British Columbia by keeping the procurement in Canada, ordered his officials to cancel the July 14 briefing with the foreign firms and demanded to know why DND was not considering a Canadian firm.

Bureaucrats in National Defence Headquarters (NDHQ) responded to the minister's demand with an amendment that removed the exclusion of developmental vehicles. In February 1999, the change was made formally, in "order to foster a greater degree of direct participation by Canadian industry." This change further delayed the competition; in the end, the final bids did not close until May 2001 — fully three and a half years after Treasury Board approval.

But in that time, the landscape had changed dramatically. Ironically, Western Star was no longer in the picture. The firm had been sold in 2000 to Freightliner Corporation of Portland, Oregon, a division of Daimler Trucks North America, which in turn was a subsidiary of Daimler AG. In August 2000, Western Star announced that it was withdrawing its M1044 from the LUVW competition, not surprising given that Mercedes-Benz, one of the other competitors, was a multinational division of Daimler AG. (In October 2001, Freightliner announced that, as part of a rationalization, all of Western Star's production would be moved to a new $16 million production facility in Portland; the Kelowna plant would be closed, with the loss of 675 jobs.)

Moreover, Eggleton's political interference in 1998, which had sent the unmistakeable signal that Western Star was going to get the contract, had prompted both Land Rover and AM General to withdraw from the competition. In particular, AM General's strong global market position meant that it had no interest in setting up an assembly plant in Canada, one of the conditions that the Canadian government was demanding of the successful bidder. AM General was successfully selling Humvees to armed forces around the world, and no other country was demanding that the company establish a local assembly line as a condition of the sale.

That left the Mercedes-Benz Gelandwagen as the sole remaining competitor. The formal bid, submitted by DaimlerChrysler, together with DEW Engineering of Ottawa, was eventually judged to be the compliant, lowest-cost bid, and a contract was signed in October 2003, with deliveries between March 2004 and August 2005. In the meantime, a contract for COTS vehicles for service in Canada had already been signed in October 2002 with General Motors Canada for delivery of eight hundred militarized Silverados.

By the time that Cpl. Beerenfenger, Sgt. Short, and Cpl. Murphy were killed, Eggleton was no longer minister of national defence. Caught up in the bitter internal feud between Jean Chrétien and Paul Martin over the party leadership, he had been dropped from cabinet by Chrétien in May 2002. The nominal reason was that he had been caught violating conflict-of-interest guidelines by hiring his girlfriend to do research; the real reason was that Eggleton was supporting Martin's push for Chrétien to resign. (Indeed, Martin quit Chrétien's cabinet the week after Eggleton was sacked.) For the remainder of the 37th Parliament, Eggleton sat on the Liberal backbench; he was able to leave it to others to explain why Canadians had been sent to Afghanistan with the soft-skinned Iltis jeeps. Happily for him, no one ever called him out on his interference in the procurement process in 1998 that caused the long delay in providing Canadian troops in Afghanistan with a replacement. In 2005, Paul Martin, prime minister at last, appointed Eggleton to the Senate.

THE *VICTORIA*-CLASS SUBMARINES

The Royal Canadian Navy (RCN) acquired a small submarine fleet in the early 1960s, driven in large part by the expansion of the Cold War under the ocean surface.[25] Canada's contribution to submarine warfare was modest: in 1961, an ex–U.S. Navy submarine was leased from the United States and used exclusively for anti-submarine warfare training; in 1968, this training submarine was replaced by another former American submarine. In 1962, three British *Oberon*-class submarines were ordered by the Diefenbaker government and entered service between 1965 and 1967, based in Halifax.

Planning for the replacement of the *Oberon*-class submarines began in the early 1980s, and during the Mulroney era there was a brief consideration of replacing these diesel-electric submarines with nuclear-powered submarines. The 1987 defence white paper committed the government to the purchase of twelve nuclear submarines, but in 1989 the program was cancelled both because of cost and because public opinion was opposed to the nuclear option. In 1990, a non-nuclear-powered option was resurrected by the Maritime Command (as the RCN was known between 1968 and 2011).

In the meantime, the Royal Navy (RN) in the United Kingdom had decided to mothball its small fleet of four *Upholder*-class submarines. Designed in the 1970s and built between 1986 and 1993, these diesel-electric submarines were intended to supplement the RN's nuclear submarine force. They saw limited service before the British government decided that it was going to move to an all nuclear-powered fleet. So the four submarines were decommissioned between 1992 and 1994 and put in long-term storage in Barrow-in-Furness while the British government looked for a buyer. Canada was one of eight countries to whom the U.K. Ministry of Defence pitched the subs. In August 1995, Maritime Command presented its case for purchasing the *Upholder*-class fleet to cabinet. Negotiations between the two navies resulted in a proposal by NDHQ to the Chrétien cabinet to purchase the four submarines and a suite of "trainers" (training simulator units) for $750 million.

In April 1998, cabinet agreed to the purchase. The Chrétien government had finally balanced the budget, and the continuation of a submarine capability had been bruited as an option in its 1994 defence white paper. The *Oberon*-class submarines were at the very end of their service lives and by 2000 would no longer be safe to operate. The price was heralded as a substantial bargain, since it was estimated that a comparable fleet of new submarines and trainers would cost $3 billion to $5 billion. As Chrétien's defence minister, Art Eggleton, admitted, the government would not have been willing to spend that kind of money to purchase new submarines.

The boats were refitted at Barrow by BAE Systems and then handed over to Canada between 2000 and 2004. The new submarines were renamed after Canadian port cities and reclassified as the *Victoria*-class, after the first submarine to enter Canadian service, HMCS *Victoria*. Once in Canadian possession, the submarines needed considerable repair and refit work, much related to the fact that the submarines had been kept in saltwater storage for so long. Cracks were found in some of the valves, and some high-pressure welds had to be replaced. Because the submarines had been put into storage with water in their fuel tanks, some steel piping also had to be replaced. In addition, the boats had to be "Canadianized" to meet navy requirements: a new torpedo fire-control system, the Lockheed Martin Librascope, was installed, and the torpedo tubes were refitted to enable the submarines to fire the Gould Mk 48 heavyweight torpedoes that were used by the *Oberon*-class and that Canada had in store. A new UHF satellite communications system was installed. Some of the weapons systems of the *Upholder*-class were removed.

Once transferred to Canadian service, however, the submarines were plagued by a series of malfunctions and loss of operational capacity. On October 5, 2004, three days after it had been accepted by the Canadian navy, HMCS *Chicoutimi* was making its maiden voyage to Halifax. A loose upper vent in the conning tower needed fixing, and the captain decided to leave the hatches open rather than "lock out" the technicians working on the tower. As these repairs were being undertaken on the surface in rough seas, a rogue wave hit the submarine, dumping some two thousand litres of seawater through the open hatch. An arc in power cables immersed in water caused a fire, which killed Lieut. Chris Saunders and injured nine others. *Chicoutimi* was towed back to Scotland and subsequently sealifted to Esquimalt, where repairs on the severely damaged electrical system took ten years and cost approximately $125 million. Not until September 2014 did the submarine undergo sea trials.

HMCS *Victoria* had to be pulled from service when its electrical system was destroyed in 2004 as a result of it being hooked up to an on-shore electrical supply in error. It was then sent for a refit in dry dock between 2005 and 2011 and not declared fully operational until 2012. HMCS *Windsor* underwent a five-year refit that took it out of service from 2007 until 2012, but it still suffered a defect in one of its diesel generators that restricted its operations. HMCS *Corner Brook* had no comparable difficulties: it was the one submarine in operational service from 2003 until June 2011, when, as a result of human error, it ran aground, severely damaging its bow. It underwent repairs and then began its regular "deep maintenance" cycle, taking it out of service until 2018.

In 2008, an in-service contract worth $1.5 billion for the maintenance of the submarine fleet was awarded to Babcock Canada. However, a significant problem has emerged since then: it is increasingly difficult to secure spare parts for the submarines, since the original manufacturers went out of business long ago. Unlike the *Oberon*-class submarines, which had an established supply claim for the twenty-seven submarines being operated by six navies, only four *Upholder*-class submarines were built, rendering it an "orphan class" submarine. The difficulty of securing access to spare parts has caused the cost of maintenance to increase, particularly as the submarines age.

The various problems encountered by the *Victoria*-class submarines gave them a distinctly poor reputation in Canada. The criticism was particularly stoked by a British MP, Mike Hancock, who represented Portsmouth, where the *Upholder*-class submarines had been based before they were decommissioned. In a widely publicized interview in March 2012, Hancock claimed that Canada had been "daft" to buy the submarines and Britain had been wrong to do a "dumb deal" with an ally like Canada. As he put it, "'Buyer beware' should have been painted on the sides of these submarines." He later disclosed a letter he had received from Britain's junior minister of defence, Peter Luff, that revealed that in 2002 and 2004 the Canadian government had been sufficiently concerned about the condition of the submarines that it had demanded some compensation. While no compensation was paid, Luff wrote Hancock in April, the price of the final submarine was reduced by £2 million "as an act of good faith and without liability." Hancock was not shy about sharing his reactions with Canadians. "It just shows you how badly Canada was shafted," he said. "They flog you some dead ducks of submarines and won't give you compensation and then give you £2 million to go away and be quiet."[26] Hancock's comments were seized on by some critics who sought to use the maintenance issues to try to delegitimize the submarines to support their argument that a submarine role of the CAF was no longer necessary.[27]

Finally, in early 2015, the submarine fleet was declared fully "operational" — in other words, three of the four submarines were available for operations. However, getting a fully operational status for Canada's submarine fleet had taken just under seventeen years since the Chrétien government approved the purchase in 1998. The second-hand submarines had also consumed considerably more of the defence budget than had been originally thought when the Chrétien cabinet had been so attracted by the $750 million bargain on offer from the British.

These stories demonstrate how difficult it has been for Canadian policymakers to get Williams's formula — the right equipment, at the right time, in the right place, with the right support, and at the right price — right. The historical procurements surveyed in this chapter were messes, as we have defined that term in the introduction, and indeed, in the case of the Ross rifle, the mess directly caused the deaths of unknown numbers of Canadian troops on the Western Front who were sent into battle with a weapon that did not work properly.

We now turn to two contemporary messes that are ongoing. In these procurements — the replacements of two aging aircraft, the CH-124 Sea King helicopter and the CF-18 Hornet fighter — virtually everything that could go wrong in the quest to get the right equipment at the right time and at the right price has gone wrong.

2

GETTING IT *ALL* WRONG:
THE SEA KING AND F-35 FIASCOS

There are two programs that epitomize the failure of defence procurement in Canada. One is the replacement for the shipborne CH-124 Sea King helicopters that were acquired beginning in 1963. The other is the aborted program to replace the aging CF-18 Hornet fighter jets that have been in service since 1982. These two programs are such fiascos — in the classical meaning of that Italian word — that they need to be surveyed separately. As will become evident, these two programs are truly "poster" projects for Canada's procurement failures.

THE SEA KING FIASCO

The attempt to replace the Sikorsky CH-124 Sea King shipborne helicopters is Canada's longest-running military procurement.[1] The Sea Kings entered service in the early 1960s, primarily but not exclusively in an anti-submarine warfare

(ASW) role, and deployed on Canada's lone aircraft carrier, HMCS *Bonaventure,* as well as on the navy's destroyers and destroyer escorts. Because they had been designed in the 1950s, the Sea Kings were increasingly ineffective in ASW operations in the 1970s, even with upgrades. So planners in the Department of National Defence started to discuss what features a replacement helicopter would need: a Statement of Requirements (SOR) was agreed on in 1975, and a Sea King Replacement Program was registered in the Defence Capital Program in July 1978, renamed the New Shipborne Aircraft (NSA) program in 1981.

The Progressive Conservative government of Brian Mulroney formally approved the search for a replacement on August 5, 1986, and a request for proposals (RFP) was issued. In February 1987, two European companies responded. EH Industries (short for European Helicopter Industries), a joint venture between Agusta, an Italian aeronautics company, and Westland Helicopters, a British firm, proposed the EH101 (it was supposed to have been the EHI01, but an initial handwritten transcription error rendered it as EH101 and the designation stuck). The EH101 was a three-engine British–Italian design that was being developed by the Royal Navy in Britain and the Italian navy, the Marina Militare, to replace the Sea Kings in service in those two navies. Aérospatiale, a French state-owned aerospace manufacturer, proposed its AS332 Super Puma, which had been designed in the 1950s as a land-support helicopter.

The Canadian procurement evaluation decided that the EH101 was the only one of the two helicopters that fully met the requirements. In addition, the package of economic benefits being proposed by EH Industries, which had a regional balance between firms in Halifax, Montreal, and Ottawa, was judged to be superior to that proposed by Aérospatiale, which was concentrated overwhelmingly in Quebec. In April 1988, the Mulroney government selected EH Industries as the sole source for the completion of the project; this was followed by a protracted series of negotiations between EH Industries and DND on the precise details of the final contract, so that it was not until March 1992 that EH Industries put its final proposal to the government. On July 24, the minister of national defence, Marcel Masse, announced the $4.4 billion deal in Halifax; on October 8, EH Industries, its prime Canadian partner, Paramax Systems of Montreal, and the Canadian government signed the contract.

One of the reasons for the delay was that the program had been expanded. In the late 1980s, Canada's fifteen search-and-rescue (SAR) helicopters, the Boeing Vertol CH-113 Labradors, which had entered service at the same time as the Sea Kings in the early 1960s, were coming to the end of their lives. A New Search and Rescue Helicopter (NSH) program was created to look for a replacement for the Labradors. Because the EH101 clearly met the requirements of the NSH, DND decided that it would make sense to acquire the EH101 in two versions: thirty-five shipborne versions for naval duties and fifteen aircraft for search-and-rescue operations. Having a single aircraft perform two different functions would not only rationalize the fleet, but would also achieve savings in the capital acquisition phase, in pilot and crew training, and in maintenance and servicing over the life cycle of the aircraft.

As the contract was being finalized in 1992, however, the helicopter procurement became a high-profile political issue. The July 24 announcement was met with protests by the opposition parties. The defence critic for the New Democratic Party

(NDP), Andrew Brewin, dismissed the aircraft as a "Cold War helicopter" and argued that the acquisition was "appalling for what it says about the government's priorities." He promised that an NDP government would immediately cancel the program. His colleague, Lorne Nystrom, claimed that buying "the most expensive military helicopters in the world, the Cadillac version, is all wrong." Jean Chrétien, the leader of the opposition, also claimed that the government had "its priorities wrong."

Not surprisingly, those helicopter companies that had lost the competition joined in the protest. Boeing Canada, which had hoped to upgrade the Labradors, warned that Boeing would reassess its operations in Canada and possibly move them to the United States. Rolls-Royce criticized the decision to go with General Electric engines rather than the cheaper engines they were offering. Sikorsky Aircraft claimed that its S-92, which had been displayed as a mock-up in 1992 but which was still a "conceptual aircraft," was just as capable as the EH101 but would cost $1 billion less.[2]

The highly negative public reaction to the decision prompted the Liberals to include the helicopter procurement as part of its general attack on the Mulroney Conservatives in preparation for the election expected in 1993. Chrétien started to appropriate the NDP criticisms: he began to claim that because the Cold War was over, the threat that the helicopter was being acquired to meet — anti-submarine warfare — had ceased to exist (ignoring the large number of non-ASW operations that the Sea King had been undertaking since the end of the Cold War, most importantly surface surveillance and "vertical replenishment" of Canadian ground operations overseas). He also started to appropriate the description used by the Canadian Peace Alliance that these were "attack helicopters" that were "an obscene waste of tax dollars," and he began repeating Boeing's argument that the search-and-rescue helicopters could be upgraded for a mere $400 million. On January 27, 1993, Chrétien appropriated the NDP promise to cancel the program if a Liberal government were elected, and he even appropriated the trope first voiced by the NDP's Lorne Nystrom and began referring to the aircraft as "Cadillacs."

Needless to say, these were carefully calculated manipulations designed to paint the procurement as extravagant or militarily aggressive in a way that was putatively "un-Canadian." While the EH101 was indeed more Cadillac than it was Chevrolet, the "attack helicopter" meme was simply spurious. The phrase was clearly intended to summon images of the kind of helicopter gunships — Boeing AH-64 Apaches or Bell AH-1 Cobras — being deployed by the United States in the Persian Gulf War of 1991 or the Somalia mission that began in late 1992. While the EH101 could be outfitted with a range of attack weaponry, the version being acquired by Canada was designed for an ASW role, and thus it was armed with an ASW suite of torpedoes and a self-defence machine gun.

In the campaign to delegitimize the EH101, Chrétien chose not to mention a number of features of the procurement. He never mentioned either the anti-submarine warfare or the search-and-rescue missions when talking about the EH101. He never mentioned the other missions that the aging Sea Kings were already flying in the post–Cold War era, which the EH101 would be taking on: surface surveillance, medical evacuation, and vertical replenishment. Nor did he ever acknowledge that every study demonstrated clearly that the aging Sea Kings and Labradors would never be able to acquire modern capabilities, no matter how many upgrades they went through. Chrétien also never acknowledged the fact that Industry Canada had ranked the EH Industries offset package particularly highly. While he argued that "the economy" should be the first priority, not "defence," he never acknowledged the argument of the helicopter program's defenders that fifty thousand person-years of skilled work would be created by the offsets. And he did not mention the cost savings of having to provide in-service maintenance for just one helicopter.

The attack on the EH101s and the promise to cancel became deeply embedded in the 1993 election campaign. Kim Campbell, who had been minister of national defence before winning the leadership of the PC party and taking over as prime minister from Brian Mulroney on June 25, failed to defend the program effectively. On the contrary: Campbell implicitly acknowledged the opposition attacks by announcing in early September 1993 that the government was going to trim the procurement from fifty to forty-three. Chrétien's response was immediate: "We don't need them. We don't even need one. Forty-three is as ridiculous as fifty." And when Campbell characterized her decision to cut the seven helicopters as "the most difficult decision I have ever had to make," Chrétien countered that he would have no trouble at all making the decision to cancel: "For me, I'll take one piece of paper and I'll take my pen. I will write: 'Zero helicopters — Chrétien.' That will be it. I will not lose one minute of sleep over it."[3]

And that, indeed, was it. In the general election of October 25, 1993, the Liberals won a majority and the Progressive Conservatives were reduced to just two seats, with every minister except Jean Charest losing their seat. Chrétien and his cabinet were sworn in on November 4 and held their first cabinet meeting that very afternoon, deciding to cancel the New Shipborne

Aircraft program and the contract that had been signed the year before. The next day, Paramax had to fire 750 employees. The process of cancelling the contract took a little longer: in January 1996, the Chrétien government announced that it had cost $478.3 million to cancel the contract: $88.7 million in contract cancellation fees, $235 million for work in progress, and $154.6 million for work done in the project definition phase.[4] However, the Liberal government chose not to include an estimate of how much had been spent in labour costs of government employees who had worked on the project since 1986. While in his memoirs Chrétien spins the cancellation as a cost saving,[5] the reality is that Canadians ended up spending vastly more than $4.4 billion to acquire a helicopter capability as a consequence.

For the Sea Kings and the Labradors were getting older. Eventually Chrétien had to admit that the helicopters needed to be replaced. But to justify its overtly political decision in 1993, the government once again chose to split the helicopter replacement in two. It approved the procurement of a fleet of fifteen search-and-rescue helicopters in 1995, specifying that the winner would have to be bought off the shelf. A competition for a winning bid was held in 1996–97.

The competition was won hands-down by the EH101. Because DND realized that this decision would embarrass Chrétien, it contracted KPMG Washington, the firm that conducts all procurement audits for the U.S. Department of Defense, to conduct an independent audit. KPMG concluded that the project "was one of the best procurement evaluations we have seen."

The KPMG audit of the procurement obviously carried little weight with Chrétien or his ministers, for the cabinet worked exceedingly hard to get the DND recommendation overturned. Cabinet ordered the Department of Justice to determine if there was a way to avoid giving the contract to EH Industries. When Justice indicated that it would not be lawful to reverse such a recommendation, the Prime Minister's Office (PMO) then hired a retired Ontario judge to offer an opinion. Again, the cabinet was advised that rejecting the winning bid without cause would be highly problematic, if not illegal. Undeterred, the PMO then went to Lang Michener, a Toronto law firm, to ask if the selection process could be discredited. For a third time, cabinet was told that because the procurement had been run well, it would have to choose the EH101.

Having spent nearly $100,000 trying to find a way to avoid accepting the recommendation, the cabinet gave up. On January 5, 1998, it formally selected the EH101, though it pretended that the helicopter that was designated the CH-149 Cormorant by the CAF was a different helicopter than the EH101 that it had rejected in November 1993. While technically it was — the SAR version in the 1992 contract had been designated the CH-149 Chimo — this bit of legerdemain did not deter the press from ridiculing the Chrétien government for having wasted both time and money. Indeed, in an assessment of the winners and losers in the helicopter procurement, Hugh Winsor of the *Globe and Mail* opined that Chrétien was "heading the list of losers."[6] However, as Aaron Plamondon has pointed out,[7] whatever negative fallout this decision might have generated was completely overshadowed by a massive ice storm that hit eastern Canada quite literally at the very moment that the EH101 decision was being announced. As the minister of national defence, Art Eggleton, was making his formal announcement in Ottawa, a steady freezing rain that would last for eighty hours was falling in eastern

Ontario and southern Quebec. The accumulated ice downed hundreds of thousands of trees and caused the widespread destruction of the electrical infrastructure and the extended loss of power for hundreds of thousands of customers. Almost sixteen thousand Canadian troops were deployed to assist in the crisis.

While the ice storm saved his government from embarrassment on the search-and-rescue replacement, Prime Minister Chrétien did not make the same mistake twice. The search for a replacement for the Sea Kings was heavily torqued by the PMO to ensure that the EH101 could not possibly win that competition. First, both the SOR and the accompanying "requirement specifications" were downgraded and diluted so that a range of other helicopters could meet the requirements. While initially there were 1,400 mandatory technical requirements, these were progressively removed by DND at the urging of the PMO. By the time the competitors' bids were evaluated, there were only 475 requirements. Moreover, bidders were allowed to just give their word that they would comply with the other requirements.

Most important was the change that allowed a developmental aircraft to compete. Had the original requirement of an off-the-shelf purchase been kept, the Sikorsky S-92 would not have been considered, since that aircraft did not yet exist and would have to be developed for Canada. But in 2003, the rules were changed to allow a developmental aircraft. Second, the procurement was divided into two parts — one company would be contracted to build the airframe and another to manufacture the avionics and mission systems. This tactic was adopted to ensure that AgustaWestland International (as EH Industries had become in 2000) could not claim savings that might be realized by procuring the same helicopter as the SAR fleet. Although this was eventually reversed, it was a telling indication of just how far the Chrétien cabinet was willing to go to ensure that the EH101 would fail.

Finally, cabinet insisted on a "lowest-cost compliant" bid that required that the lowest cost proposed had to be accepted, provided that the aircraft and package was "compliant." This was a clear violation of Treasury Board contracting rules that required that procurements secure "best value," which was defined as "the consideration of all relevant costs over the useful life of the acquisition, not solely the initial or basic contractual cost." But for the Chrétien cabinet, following the rules was clearly less important than ensuring that the EH101 would not win.

In addition to these various obstacles placed in Agusta Westland's way, a third factor was working against the EH101 and in favour of competitors: the enforced glacial pace of the Maritime Helicopter Project. The initial SOR was signed off by the chief of the defence staff in the summer of 1999. Formal cabinet approval for the replacement was given on August 17, 2000. But the RFP was not posted until November 2001. The deadline for bids kept being pushed back, so that it was not until December 17, 2003, that the RFP was formally approved and companies were required to submit "fully compliant" pre-qualification proposals. While Alan Williams, who was the ADM (materiel) during this period, criticizes the long delay between the SOR and the RFP as "mostly just time wasted,"[8] he diplomatically does not mention that the delay was driven for entirely political reasons: the longer the process was strung out, the likelier it was that there would be "lowest-cost compliant" competitors to the EH101 and that it would not be Jean Chrétien who was the prime minister when the final helicopter decision was taken.

For the bitter civil war between Chrétien and Martin and their respective supporters over the Liberal party leadership in 2003 also affected the Sea King program. Chrétien was annoyed at Martin's efforts to push him out, and so he took his sweet time in stepping down: in August 2002, Chrétien announced that he would not resign until February 2004. The campaign to succeed Chrétien consumed the energy of Liberal MPs, including members of cabinet, for much of 2003. While Martin was elected leader on November 14, almost a month went by before Chrétien formally stepped down and Martin was sworn in as prime minister on December 12.

The infighting within the Chrétien government had an important impact on the helicopter replacement. The three-engine EH101 remained the strongest contender for the shipborne helicopter. It was in service with other navies, and its search-and-rescue variant was already in service in Canada, ensuring that maintenance costs would be lower than if there were two different fleets. The other primary contender, the Sikorsky S-92, was still a "paper aircraft." But as long as Chrétien remained in power, there were strong reasons to keep deferring a decision so that he would not suffer the kind of embarrassment that he surely would have suffered in 1998 had the ice storm not intervened.

Even though Chrétien was no longer prime minister, the fix was already in: a contract with Sikorsky was signed in 2004 for the CH-148 Cyclone, a military version of the civilian S-92 that still had to be specially developed for the CAF. While the first deliveries of the fleet of twenty-eight Cyclones were supposed to begin in 2008, with all helicopters due to be delivered in 2011, a series of glitches kept delaying the deliveries. The Conservatives, who had inherited the program, became more frustrated. Peter MacKay, the minister of national defence, went so far as to openly declare that the Sikorsky acquisition was "the worst procurement in the history of Canada."[9]

However, the Conservative government could not bring itself to take any action against Sikorsky. It could have demanded $89 million in late delivery penalties but chose not to act. And while the government threatened to look at other options in 2013, it was clearly unwilling to walk away from the Sikorsky deal and, for example, buy a fleet of Cormorants off the shelf for the maritime helicopter. Instead, the Conservatives reopened the contract with Sikorsky for a third time and renegotiated a deal that was even sweeter for Sikorsky, with even softer delivery deadlines.

Finally, in June 2015, fully forty years after the initial SOR for the Sea King was written, the first block of six Cyclones was delivered to Halifax to begin the process of phasing out the aging Sea Kings. But even while Conservative ministers were staging self-congratulatory photo-ops in Halifax, the Maritime Helicopter Project office in DND was worrying that the Cyclone's engines "will not deliver the power required to meet all critical performance requirements."[10] And, if Sikorsky actually makes the final deliveries on schedule, the last Cyclones will not be delivered until 2021, many years behind schedule and at least $200 million over budget.

THE F-35 FIASCO

What should have been a relatively straightforward, even if highly complex, defence procurement decision — replacing Canada's fleet of aging CF-18 Hornets — also turned into a fiasco, though not as long-running as the Sea King saga.[11]

The story of Canada's F-35 acquisition began in 1997, when the Chrétien government decided to join an American-led multi-national consortium that would produce a new Joint Strike Fighter (JSF). The JSF was the result of an important decision by the U.S. Congress in 1994 that the U.S. Air Force, the U.S. Navy, and the U.S. Marine Corps should all fly just one fighter (hence *Joint* Strike Fighter) that was designed to be able to deliver all the traditional roles of fighter aircraft: air-to-air and air-to-ground attack, ground/naval strike, aerial surveillance, air-superiority/interception, and also have what is known as "swing-role" capability (the ability to instantly change roles while flying on a sortie). To reduce costs, the U.S. created an international partnership of American allies. Each partner would invest in the program, and each ally's aerospace firms would eventually participate in the global value chains created by the program. In 1996, Boeing and Lockheed Martin were chosen as the two firms to compete for the winner-take-all contract.

In January 1998, the Chrétien government formally joined the United States and seven other countries — Australia, Britain, Denmark, Italy, The Netherlands, Norway, and Turkey — and signed the "concept demonstration" phase of the program. As a "Level 3" participant, Canada invested approximately US$440 million, with the expectation that Canadian aerospace firms would receive contracts from whichever company won the competition. In 2001, Lockheed Martin's F-35 Lightning II was chosen by the United States, and in February 2002, the Chrétien government signed on to the next phase of the program, the "system development and demonstration" phase. After the Conservatives under Stephen Harper took power in February 2006, they committed Canada to the next phase, the "production, sustainment and follow-on development" phase, in December 2006.

Joining the JSF program in 1998 and committing to the next phases in 2002 and 2006 were logical decisions, both economically and strategically. While the Chrétien government might have been more attracted by the benefits to Canada's aerospace sector that would come from being in Lockheed Martin's global value chains than the military benefits of the F-35 itself, the F-35 was also a strategically sound choice. Simply put: if the F-35 was the only fighter that the U.S. armed forces were going to be flying in the 2020s and 2030s, then it was a logical fighter for Canada. Since the cancellation of the CF-105 Arrow in 1959, Canadians have only flown American-built fighters. It was thus anticipated that the F-35, being the only American fighter-interceptor in production, would eventually replace the CF-18.

The usual next step would have been to launch a formal replacement program for the CF-18 Hornet. Instead, the Harper government was persuaded by National Defence Headquarters (NDHQ) to do what the Australians had done in 2002 and move directly to acquiring the F-35 as a sole-source contract without bothering with a competition. After all, the air force had determined that Canada needed stealth capability, which only "fifth-generation" fighters had.* And the F-35 was the only

---

* The evolution of jet fighters is usually characterized in "generations." First-generation fighters (mid-1940s to mid-1950s) were subsonic aircraft; they had no radar and only unguided munitions. Second-generation fighters (mid-1950s to early 1960s) were capable of supersonic flight and had air-to-air radar and guided missiles. Third-generation fighters (early 1960s to 1970) were multi-role fighters and had beyond-visual-range homing missiles. Fourth-generation fighters (1970 to late 1980s), such as the CF-18 Hornet, featured heads-up display, fly-by-wire technology, and "swing-role" capability (able to change roles instantly; e.g., from air-to-air to air-to-ground). Fifth-generation fighters like the F-22 and F-35 featured stealth capacity, advanced avionics, and high manoeuvrability. Some advanced versions of fourth-generation fighters, such as

fifth-generation fighter available on the market (the U.S. government was not permitting the only other fifth-generation stealth fighter in existence, the Lockheed Martin F-22 Raptor, to be sold abroad, not even to close allies). Since there was no competition, the thinking went, there was no need for a competition. So, in its 2008 defence white paper, the *Canada First Defence Strategy*, the Harper government promised that, as part of its recapitalization program for the CAF, it would acquire sixty-five "next-generation fighters" — which could only be the F-35, since it was the only other "next-generation" fighter on the market (the only other fifth-generation fighters in development at the time were the Russian Sukhoi PAK FA and Chinese Chengdu J-20 fighters, both highly unlikely candidates for a Canadian procurement).

Two years later, on July 16, 2010, the Harper government finally announced that it had approved the purchase of a fleet of sixty-five F-35s. There would be no competition to replace the CF-18s; the contract would be untendered and sole-sourced. The cost of the F-35s, the government ministers at the announcement claimed, would be $9 billion.

The Conservatives did not try to offer a plausible strategic rationale for the F-35. They did not try to explain why sixty-five next-generation fighters were needed for the CAF. No effort was made to explain the "generational" changes that were occurring in fighter aircraft and why "fourth-generation" aircraft like the CF-18 Hornet badly needed to be replaced. And why sixty-five? In 1980, Canada had needed 130 fighters; what had changed?

---

the Boeing F-18 Super Hornet, Eurofighter Typhoon, Saab Gripen, and Dassault Rafale, are known as "4.5-generation" fighters because they have some stealth technology and feature radar-absorbing materials, thrust vectoring, active phased array radar, and "swing-role" capability.

No effort was made to explain what was happening to jet fighter production lines in the United States: that by the 2020s and 2030s, there was going to be only one fighter being produced, and that would be the F-35. All other fighters currently in production, such as so-called 4.5-generation fighters like the Boeing F/A-18 Super Hornet and the Advanced Super Hornet, would likely be closing their production lines, even though these aircraft could be maintained in service until the late 2030s.

Instead, the Conservatives simply politicized the procurement. Seeing the F-35 as a useful way to boost their political fortunes, they played political games with justifications that were, in a word, nonsensical. For example, the Harper government claimed that the periodic intrusions of Russian Federation Tupolev TU-95 bombers — known as Bears in the West — into Canadian airspace in the Arctic demonstrated why Canada needed new F-35s; a similar claim was made about Canada's participation in NATO air strikes in Libya in 2011.[12] In each case, the claim was spurious. Even though the USAF usually scrambles its stealthy F-22 Raptors to counter Russian provocations in its airspace, one does not need anything more advanced than a fourth-generation fighter such as the CF-18 to counter propeller-driven Bears. And while eventually fighters with fifth-generation capabilities will indeed be needed to counter the new generation of Russian bombers presently in development, that argument was never made by the Harper government. In the case of the Libyan intervention in 2011, the fact that the U.S. used every airplane in its inventory *except* its stealthy F-22 demonstrated clearly that one did not need stealth capabilities for that kind of mission.

Even the announcement of the sole-source procurement was politicized. Rather than making the announcement in

Parliament, the F-35 decision was unambiguously used as a political prop: in a classic case of "government by photo-op," a model F-35 was trucked to Ottawa from Texas by Lockheed Martin so that Peter MacKay, the minister of national defence, could be photographed in the cockpit giving a smiling thumbs-up on a Friday afternoon in July.

Most importantly, however, the Conservative government did not try to ensure that the Liberals, who had committed Canada to the F-35 partnership in the first place, were on board. Instead, the politicization of the CF-18 replacement by the Conservatives prompted the Liberal opposition to return the favour. Even though they had committed Canada to the JSF in the first place, the Liberals now sought to politicize the F-35 and delegitimize the aircraft as a means of bashing the Conservatives. Some of the Liberal criticism focused on the F-35 itself, with the Liberals asking whether Canada really needed a complex, sophisticated, and expensive aircraft like the F-35; some criticism focused on the sole-sourcing decision, with the Liberal leader, Michael Ignatieff, promising in October 2010 that if a Liberal government were elected in the elections expected in 2011, it would cancel the F-35 and hold an "open competition" for a new fighter aircraft.[13]

But most of the Liberal critique fixed on cost. In the July 2010 announcement, the Harper government had claimed that the F-35s would cost $9 billion, even though documents leaked to the *Globe and Mail* the month before had revealed that DND had estimated that an additional $6.93 billion in "sustainment services" and $9.6 billion in operating costs would be needed over twenty years.[14]

Faced with different definitions of "cost," the Liberals saw an opportunity to expose the government's inconsistent narrative on the price of the F-35. They decided to bring the parliamentary budget officer, a new position that had been created by the Conservatives in 2006, into the process. The PBO, Kevin Page, released his report in March 2011. Page provided a very different set of figures. While DND was using a twenty-year life cycle to calculate costs, Page argued that a more appropriate life cycle was thirty years; after all, the CF-18s would be over thirty years old by the time they were retired. And while the government was claiming that each F-35 fighter aircraft would cost US$75 million, the PBO, using a different methodology to forecast jet fighter costs, calculated that in fact each plane would cost US$148 million. The PBO concluded that the total program cost would be $29.3 billion.[15]

The dispute over the "real" cost of the F-35 quickly became part of a larger dispute between the Harper Conservatives and the opposition in the minority 40th Parliament over the release of financial information to Parliament. When the Harper government refused to release the information, the opposition parties in the House of Commons declared the government to be in contempt of Parliament and brought it down by a motion of non-confidence on March 25, 2011.

While the F-35 was not an issue in the election campaign that followed, the question of the F-35's cost dogged the Conservatives after they were returned with a majority in the May 2011 elections. Michael Ferguson, the auditor general, also audited the F-35 program. In April 2012, Ferguson released his report on the fighter replacement program.[16] It found that the procurement process had been inappropriately run by both DND and Public Works and Government Services Canada (PWGSC), with DND submitting documentation to cabinet that was either out of sequence or incomplete. For example, the defence procurement process normally begins with a Statement of Requirements that outlines what the equipment must be able to do. In the case of the F-35, the SOR was dated June 1, 2010, fully two years *after* the Harper government announced in the *Canada First Defence Strategy* that it would acquire sixty-five next-generation fighters. Likewise, because DND wanted to acquire the F-35 without running an open competition, it was required to seek an exemption under the Government Contracts Regulations that require an open competition for large capital projects. But PWGSC was not given the justificatory documents by DND until August 2010, the month *after* the July 2010 announcement by the Harper government that it was acquiring the aircraft. The only justification for sole-sourcing the project was a letter, provided on the very same day that it was requested by PWGSC, confirming that DND needed a fifth-generation fighter aircraft and that the F-35 was the only aircraft that met that requirement. According to the auditor general, the June 1, 2010, letter contained no other supporting documents.

The auditor general's report also focused on the cost projections, noting that DND understated the costs. Like the parliamentary budget officer, the auditor general wondered why DND was using a twenty-year life cycle rather than a "full" life cycle, which was, in his view, at least thirty-six years, suggesting that the "real cost" of the F-35 fleet would be closer to $36 billion.

The conclusions of the report contained a devastating indictment of both DND and PWGSC. National Defence, the auditor general claimed, did not exercise due diligence in managing the process. It did not consult PWGSC as it should have; it did not inform cabinet fully; and it did not provide "timely and complete documentation" to support its recommendations. For its part, PWGSC did not exercise due diligence either, simply accepting whatever DND told it "in the absence of required documentation and completed analysis."

The auditor general's report was released to the public on April 3, 2012. The response of the Harper government (which of course had had prior access to the report) was immediate and draconian. That same day, the funding envelope for the F-35 acquisition was frozen. The management of the program was taken away from DND and put in the hands of a newly created secretariat located in PWGSC.[17] The Harper government also called in KPMG to conduct an independent audit.

KPMG conducted its audit in the fall of 2012. The auditors concluded that all the previous life-cycle assumptions were wrong and that a forty-two-year life cycle should be used. On that basis, the full life-cycle cost of the F-35 program would be $45.8 billion. As that figure started leaking out, the Harper government began putting what Jeffrey Simpson has called its "spin machine" into reverse.[18] On November 22, Rona Ambrose, the minister of public works, promised to "look at all the options" for the replacement, including asking the manufacturers of other fighter aircraft to submit expressions of interest.[19] Although there was a flurry of speculation after a cabinet committee meeting in early December that the government was going to cancel the program altogether — "F-35 Dead in the Air" was the headline on the front page of the print version of the *National Post* on December 7 — in fact, what the Harper government decided on was widely called a "reset": start the process of replacing the CF-18s from the beginning.[20]

There was, of course, a perfectly good reason why it looked as though the price had jumped from $9 billion to $45.8 billion in just thirty months. The original very palatable figure of $9 billion had been just the "fly-away" cost, without any "life-cycle" costs. Moreover, if the length of the life cycle is changed, that will affect the "full life-cycle cost" of a weapons system. The CAF, the PBO, the auditor general, and KPMG were all using different definitions of the F-35's life cycle. But "real cost" remained relatively unchanged: whether over twenty, thirty, thirty-six, or forty-two years, the full cost of the F-35 was always going to be approximately $1 billion per year.

Needless to say, however, serving up that explanation would have required that the Harper government explain why it had seemingly not been up-front about the "full life-cycle costs" from the beginning and why it had seemingly been trying to pull a fast one in July 2010 by claiming that Canada would be getting a new F-35 fleet for just $9 billion.

So the Conservatives just gave up and backed away from the program altogether. With the "reset," the CF-18 replacement process was back at the beginning. And in the thirty-four months between the 2012 reset and the defeat of the Conservatives in the October 2015 elections, there was very little progress on the replacement of the CF-18. The "F-35 Secretariat" was renamed the "National Fighter Procurement Secretariat," and the "next generation fighter" project was symbolically redubbed the "future fighter capability" (proving once again that someone in the defence procurement system had a sense of humour — since, with the reset, the CF-18 replacement was indeed far into the future). In its annual report on Major Crown Projects in 2015, DND reported that Treasury Board approval would not be expected until 2018–20, with delivery of a replacement for the CF-18 fleet simply listed as

"TBD" — to be determined. Instead, the Harper government announced in September 2014 that it would upgrade the existing CF-18 fleet to extend its life to 2025.

The election of the Liberals in 2015 introduced a further element of uncertainty into the replacement program. Even after the 2012 reset, the Liberals consistently maintained their opposition to the F-35. Indeed, the new Liberal leader, Justin Trudeau, went well beyond the promise of his predecessor, Michael Ignatieff, that a Liberal government would start the process over. On September 20, 2015, in the middle of the election campaign, Trudeau announced that a Liberal government would run an "open competition" to replace the CF-18, adding, albeit without any evident irony, that in this "open" competition, the F-35 would not be allowed to compete. For Trudeau promised that a Liberal government would not be acquiring the F-35, period. All the savings from choosing a putatively cheaper aircraft, Trudeau promised, would be diverted to the navy.

Once in power, Trudeau moved to make good his promise. Having "pulled a Chrétien" in the 2015 election, the Trudeau government did to the F-35 what the Chrétien government did to the EH101 after 1993: it found ways to torque the process to ensure that some other fighter — any other fighter — than the F-35 bubbled to the top of the selection process. No doubt government lawyers told the new prime minister that trying to exclude the F-35 from an "open" competition would open the government to a multi-billion-dollar lawsuit, for Trudeau did not repeat this rash promise in his mandate letter to the new minister of national defence, Harjit Sajjan. However, the Trudeau government did try to make sure that the promise that Canada would not acquire the F-35 was implemented. In

June 2016, Trudeau continued the five-year Liberal tradition of trying to delegitimize the F-35, confidently assuring the House of Commons that it was a plane that "does not work and is a long way from ever working." At the same time, the government began floating the idea that the CF-18s were so old that there would be an "unacceptable" capability gap. The proposed solution was the purchase of a small fleet of Boeing F/A-18 Super Hornets, but on a sole-source basis so that no "open" competition would have to be run. This was to be an "interim" measure, with the "final" decision on the CF-18 replacement pushed down the road.[21] But within a few weeks, the Trudeau government had abandoned that idea. On July 6, Sajjan announced that a decision to purchase Super Hornets had, in fact, not been made. Instead, the government would "seek up-to-date information from leading manufacturers on key issues, including cost, economic benefits for Canada, and their ability to deliver planes quickly." Sajjan claimed that that information would "inform a decision on a procurement path in the coming months"[22] — in other words, whether there would be an open competition or whether the government would proceed with a sole-source contract.

In the meantime, the government quietly paid US$32.9 million to the F-35 program office in the United States in late June in order to keep Canada in good standing in the multinational consortium.[23] But the gamesmanship around the Super Hornet in the summer of 2016 simply extends the fiasco created by the Conservatives. If the Trudeau government's "final" decision on the CF-18 replacement is to not acquire the F-35, it is a virtual certainty that Canadian firms will be excluded from the Lockheed Martin global value chains for this fighter. And if the Super Hornet is the only aircraft that the RCAF is fly-ing in the 2020s, this will have profound strategic consequences for Canada. The Super Hornet is not fully interoperable with fifth-generation fighters like the F-35 and F-22 Raptors flown by the USAF, posing serious questions about a future Canadian role in North American air defence. Moreover, all of the other allied air forces that operate in the Arctic — the USAF and the Danish and Norwegian air forces — operate F-35s.[24]

Now it is possible that a future government may decide to acquire F-35s for service in North American air defence, with the "interim" Super Hornet fleet deployed for those missions that do not require fifth-generation capabilities. This would make some considerable strategic sense, but it would be ex-ceedingly costly. Operating and maintaining fleets of two dif-ferent kinds of fighter aircraft would place considerable strains on Canadian defence budgets well into the future. Moreover, if Canadian firms are shut out of Lockheed Martin's global value chains as a result of a decision by the Trudeau government to go with another aircraft, there is little guarantee that these firms could be "added back" to those chains in the future.

In short, the decision of the Liberals to play politics with the CF-18 replacement during the 2015 election campaign has exacerbated the botched procurement process under the Harper Conservatives and ensured the continuation of the program's difficulties. While the F-35 fiasco has not yet reached the iconic proportions of the Sea King replacement program triggered by Chrétien's cancellation in 1993, there is little doubt that the Liberals under Justin Trudeau have put in place the makings of a major failed procurement that Canadians will be paying for, and handsomely, well into the 2020s.

❖

In the last two chapters, we have looked at six major Canadian defence procurements over the last century. The purpose has been illustrative rather than comprehensive, for over the course of Canadian history there have been a number of other major procurement failures. And it should be kept in mind that the focus has been on *major* projects. There have been thousands of minor defence procurements, the vast majority completed successfully.

We should also recognize that there have been a number of successful major procurements, where governments have been able to "get it right." Such successes would include the New Fighter Aircraft (NFA) acquisition in the late 1970s by the Liberal government of Pierre Elliott Trudeau that resulted in the acquisition of the CF-18 Hornet. There were some concerns about elements of the contract[25] and some difficulties with the fact that the CF-18s delivered to Canada were from the first production run; however, there is general agreement that the NFA program was a "model" procurement.[26]

Likewise, the acquisition of the M777 lightweight 155mm towed howitzer from BAE Systems that was begun under the Liberal government of Paul Martin and completed after the Conservative government of Stephen Harper came to power is also hailed as a highly successful project. The procurement was started in November 2005 and the guns were deployed to Kandahar by February 2006, and the Harper government acquired a further six, with options on fifteen more.[27] Two other Harper government defence procurements — the purchase of four C-17A Globemaster III strategic lift aircraft from Boeing in 2006–07 (a fifth CC-177, as the Globemaster is classified by the RCAF, was added in 2015) and the acquisition of the Boeing CH-147F Chinook medium-to-heavy lift helicopter — are also considered successes.

But against these successes must be weighed the many messy procurements; not only the historical ones examined in the previous chapter and the two fiascos examined in this chapter, but also the current record. It is telling that in 2016 every single Major Crown Project involving national defence is in difficulty, either over budget or delayed.

And as a result, Canada's military capability continues to suffer. Canada's single remaining destroyer, HMCS *Athabaskan*, was launched in 1970 and is now so old and decrepit that it had to be taken out of service in 2015 for extensive repairs. The *Victoria*-class submarines, as we noted in the previous chapter, have to have their lives extended.

Both of the navy's auxiliary oil replenishment (AOR) supply ships, commissioned in 1969–70, are no longer operational. HMCS *Protecteur* suffered a major engine room fire that completely disabled the ship in February 2014; it was decommissioned in May 2015. Even after a major refit, HMCS *Preserver* had so many problems with its electrical system and with corrosion that it was no longer able to put to sea and today sits in Halifax harbour in a state euphemistically called "extended readiness." To keep RCN ships at sea supplied, supply vessels have had to be leased from the navies of Chile and Spain. The navy cannot operate in much of the Arctic and is limited to the eastern Arctic during the short shipping season. To be sure, work has begun on new naval vessels — the Canadian surface combatant (military-speak for warships) and the Arctic/offshore patrol ships (AOPS). But there have been so many delays in cutting steel for these vessels that most will not be delivered for many years. More importantly, there is no guarantee that these naval projects will be funded into the future.

The RCAF's procurement projects have experienced similar delays. In addition to the CF-18 Hornet replacement program, the CP-140 Aurora long-range patrol aircraft fleet purchased in the 1970s was due to be replaced by a new "multi-mission" aircraft; instead, the Auroras are being upgraded to extend their service life to 2030. The RCAF was first promised a fleet of un-manned aerial vehicles (UAVs or drones) by the Conservatives during the 2005–06 election campaign, but the Joint Unmanned Surveillance Target Acquisition System (JUSTAS) — to use its formal DND name — has likewise been delayed; the first air-craft deliveries are not expected until 2021–25.

Of the three services, the Canadian Army is in the best shape, since a number of its weapons systems were renewed as a result of the army's key role in fighting during the Afghanistan mission. But even a procurement that seemed to be proceed-ing smoothly — the tactical armoured patrol vehicle (TAPV) — ran into excessive delays, and it will not be fully operation-al until 2020. Other army procurements — the close combat vehicle (CCV) and the "Medium Support Vehicle System" (aka trucks) — ran into more serious problems.

In 2009, the Conservative government announced that the army would acquire 108 close combat vehicles; these are armoured and highly mobile vehicles for infantry, essentially light tanks. In 2010, all the firms that bid on the project were disqualified; in 2012, after contending firms had spent considerable sums of money delivering prototype vehicles to be tested, the government once again rejected all the bidders. Finally, the Harper government just cancelled the CCV program in December 2013, asserting that the upgrades that had been performed on some of the light armoured vehicle (LAV) fleet would be sufficient.

The truck procurement experienced similar problems. In June 2006, an acquisition program for new medium-weight trucks for the army was announced by the new Conservative government. Two types of trucks were procured: a "militarized commercial off-the-shelf" (MilCOTS) version for use by the reserves, for training and administration, and a "standard military pattern" (SMP) truck in five variations for front-line use. The 1,300 MilCOTS were delivered beginning in 2009, with all deliveries completed by March 2011. The SMP part of the truck procurement program, by contrast, was mired in delay and controversy. The final request for proposals was not issued by DND until December 2011, fully five and a half years after the initial announcement. Officials in DND kept adding more desired capabilities to the truck, adding approximately $300 million to the cost of the procurement, but did not go back to the Treasury Board for approval to cover these additional funds.[28] It was not until July 2013 that the RFP was reissued. Finally, on July 16, 2015, nine years after the project was started, the Harper government announced that a contract had been signed with Mack Defense LLC of Allentown, Pennsylvania, for the delivery of 1,500 trucks, with delivery scheduled to begin in the summer of 2017.

In short, looking at the overall record of defence procurement in Canada today, one would be hard-pressed to argue that the defence procurement system is working well. But the stories in these two chapters are important because they put the contemporary broken procurement system in broader perspective. They remind us that what we see in 2016 has deep historical roots. These cases also suggest that when we look for ways to get it right (or at least get it "more right"), we need to understand what caused the outcomes we see in these cases, for if we are to propose the right "fixes" for defence procurement in Canada, we need to ensure that we have the causality right. To an analysis of the patterns in Canadian defence procurement we now turn.

3

EXPLAINING THE MESS

What explains the outcomes of the defence procurement decisions outlined in the previous chapters? How can we understand how Canadian governments of whatever political stripe, which have shown themselves to be competent in so many areas of public policy, appear to have had, over a long period of time, such difficulty in getting defence procurement "right"? In this chapter I look at some of the explanations for the messes we see in defence acquisition in Canada.

INSTITUTIONAL EXPLANATIONS

A common argument put forward by those seeking to explain the reasons behind the problems with military procurement in Canada is that the source for these messes can readily be located in the political and bureaucratic institutions responsible for administering the system. There are several strands to this argument.

One strand focuses on the institutional arrangements for defence procurements. The Canadian model is unique in the international system. Three separate ministers of the Crown are responsible for defence procurements: the minister of national defence, the minister in charge of the industry portfolio (at present called innovation, science and economic development), and the minister of public services and procurement. This shared authority inevitably creates significant tensions in the system, since the three ministers have very different mandates; bureaucratic politics is an inevitable consequence. As Alan Williams, a former assistant deputy minister in the Department of National Defence, has noted, his experience with this shared authority model was not a happy one, for in his view, when more than one minister is accountable for a policy area, "you have no minister accountable."[1]

Multiple lines of accountability have powerful impacts on how the system works in practice. Giving responsibility to numerous ministers inevitably slows the procurement process down, as the document trail that is integral to effective procurement becomes more difficult to negotiate. Having to secure the approvals in three separate departments, plus the approvals of the Treasury Board Secretariat, creates delays, and delays mean hugely increased costs, since defence procurement programs are always subject to what David Perry has called the "ruinous effects of inflation." As Perry notes, the cost escalation in the shipbuilding sector runs at over 11 percent a year; the Canadian surface combatant loses a $1 million in purchasing power with each day the program is delayed.[2]

Civil servants charged with overseeing defence procurement do try to speed the system up: they routinely tell their ministers that every day that a contract goes unsigned adds massively to the cost of a system. But given the shared authority, appeals to speed up the process inexorably fall on deaf ears. The lack of a singular line of accountability means that no one minister is responsible for ensuring that the process is less lackadaisical. Officials will ruefully, albeit privately, report that their ministers, already over-burdened, simply do not have the will to spend the time, energy, and political capital that would be necessary to speed up the process.

The delays encouraged by multiple lines of responsibility are exacerbated by the fact that the defence procurement bureaucracy in Canada is increasingly incapable of handling the sheer volume of business being transacted. The huge delays that we see in defence procurements, it is argued, also come from the inability of the procurement bureaucracy to process acquisitions. We have seen two interlinked developments over the last two decades. On the one hand, in the 1990s, the number of officials in DND and Public Works and Government Services Canada who worked on defence acquisition fell dramatically as the severe budget cuts of that era resulted in a slowdown in the number of capital projects and, thus, a reduced demand for those who had the specialized knowledge to be able to conduct complex acquisitions. When those officials retired and were not replaced, crucial expertise in the complexities of pricing, budgeting, and dealing with the defence industrial market was simply lost. And when the Liberal government of Paul Martin and the Conservative government of Stephen Harper decided to begin to recapitalize the armed forces in the 2000s, there simply were not enough bureaucrats with the necessary expertise available to handle the sudden surge in new procurements.

At the same time, the defence acquisition process itself became much more complex and bureaucratized, with more rigorous reporting procedures put in place, designed to enhance accountability. Of course, these changes required a greater numbers of experts in materiel management. The result was an impossible crush of defence procurement business that was being fed into a bureaucratic apparatus that not only was understaffed but also did not have the necessary expertise and experience. As David Perry noted in 2016, the Materiel Group in DND and the defence and shipbuilding secretariats at Public Services and Procurement Canada (PSPC) are so short of experienced staff that "[w]e cannot reasonably expect swift progress on $40 billion worth of projects when the team managing it is half the size of an NHL roster."[3]

Given the number of calls to dramatically increase the size of the defence procurement bureaucracy, and given the number of dollars that are returned each year by DND on procurements that have not been able to proceed on time, it can indeed be argued that one of the reasons for the dysfunction is that there are not enough bureaucrats with enough expertise in the complexities of defence procurement.

A second broad set of institutional arguments suggests that one of the reasons for the dysfunction lies specifically within the defence establishment itself — the Canadian Armed Forces and DND. In this view, many of the problems that we have seen in defence procurement can be explained by the organizational culture of the defence establishment. For example, the armed forces invariably insist that defence equipment procured must meet specifications that are often particular to the Canadian situation or particular to the CAF. For example, consider the navy's insistence that the *Victoria*-class submarines procured in 1998 had to have their fire control systems and torpedo tubes altered to fit the stock of Gould

Mk 48 torpedoes that the navy used rather than simply firing the British Spearfish torpedoes that the *Upholder*-class was designed for. As it turned out, there were solid reasons for such a modification: the Spearfish torpedoes were not only unreliable (during one test, the torpedo turned back on the submarine that had fired it), but to service them the navy would have had to ship them back to England; the Mk 48s were a proven torpedo and they were serviced in Washington state. But while, in principle, Canadianization may have sound reasoning behind it, there can be little doubt that whenever a system is modified, it tends to drive up costs and exacerbate delays.

Costs can also go up, and delays can be exacerbated, by another institutional feature that tends to be particular to smaller armed forces. Unlike large armed forces, which can afford to acquire a number of different systems for each military function, smaller armed forces have to combine different tasks into a single system.

For example, the joint support ships (JSS) that were intended to replace the auxiliary oil replenishment (AOR) ships, HMCS *Preserver* and HMCS *Protecteur*, were made more complex — and more expensive — because the navy wanted to replace the one capability of the AORs, supply and fuel replenishment, with two other capabilities: sealift and offshore command and control.

The awkward name that the defence establishment has given the next generation of warships — the "Canadian surface combatant" (CSC) — reflects the effort to replace *Iroquois*-class destroyers and *Halifax*-class frigates by using a common hull for both kinds of warships and then adapting each hull for frigate and destroyer functions.

The *Harry DeWolf*-class Arctic/offshore patrol ships (AOPS) reflect the need to combine different missions into a single procurement. The Harper government wanted naval vessels with some light ice-breaking capability to be able to "show the flag" in Canada's Arctic waters, but there is not sufficient demand for this kind of capability, so these ships will also be tasked with conducting offshore patrols in Canada's southern waters during those months of the year when the Arctic ice is too thick.

Other countries tend to acquire single-purpose systems, designing and building for the specific mission. As the JSS, CSC, and AOPS naval procurements all show, Canada has chosen not to adopt such an approach. The problem, however, is that as capabilities get added to a system, particularly if the system was not originally designed to perform those functions, the complexity of the system increases, as does its cost.

A related concern is the tendency of the defence establishment, like all bureaucracies, to organize itself so that its parochial interests are protected. Certainly one of the reasons that the F-35 procurement turned into such a fiasco was that the Harper Conservative government did not learn from the Liberal government of Pierre Elliott Trudeau that, in major defence procurements, ministers in cabinet need to control that elemental bureaucratic urge.

Trudeau *père* learned the hard way: his government was badly burned during the long-range patrol aircraft (LRPA) acquisition of the mid-1970s, when DND purposely understated the funds required, leading to the temporary cancellation of the purchase in May 1976. The LRPA acquisition was marked by what Michael Tucker has termed "bureaucratic mismanagement ensuing from ill-defined responsibilities, poor communication and misinformation."[4] Indeed, so dysfunctional was the LRPA acquisition that Trudeau's minister of supply and services, Jean-Pierre Goyer, openly accused Lawrence Stopforth, one of the senior civil servants on the LRPA project team, of "gross negligence" and of "misinforming" him, and removed him from the LRPA project. Stopforth subsequently sued Goyer for libel.[5]

But the Harper government took the view that it did not need to learn anything from the Liberals and so stumbled into the process, allowing itself to be convinced by the defence establishment to go along with its strategy for acquiring the aircraft that it wanted. The air force wanted to be flying what the Americans were flying, and — as the auditor general's 2012 report made abundantly clear — NDHQ cut all sorts of corners and played all sorts of games in its efforts to get that desired outcome.

Among these games was the well-known bureaucratic propensity to spin the costs and the capabilities of desired weapons systems to others in the procurement process — to other bureaucracies, to ministers in cabinet, and to opinion-makers. In the case of the F-35, the figure put up to the ministers was the pleasingly palatable "fly-away" figure of $9 billion, and that was the one that the ministers used in their photo-op session in July 2010.

However, it must be noted that it was the willingness of the Harper cabinet to go along with these bureaucratic games that was the true "cause" of the fiasco, not the stratagems being played out by the bureaucrats. We must look at the *principals* in the process, not the *agents*. The agents — the bureaucrats — were just doing what bureaucrats by nature do: pursue and defend their parochial organizational and professional interests, framed within a broader definition of the national interest. In principal–agent relations, however, it is the responsibility of the principals — in this case, cabinet ministers — to control the behaviour of the agents — the bureaucrats — and curb the bureaucratic games when necessary. The failure of the Harper government to impose sufficient control on the F-35 process was the real problem.

There is little doubt that one could locate some causality for the procurement mess in these institutional factors. If the present situation relating to these factors could be altered — if the lines of political authority were to be redrawn in ways similar to that of Canada's allies, if the government invested in a properly staffed procurement bureaucracy, if Canadianization could be kept to a minimum, or if the propensity of bureaucrats to be themselves could be more carefully controlled by the political leadership — it is indeed possible that one could improve some of the operations of the procurement system. It is, however, not at all clear that one would get better defence procurement, as I will argue in the following section.

THE ECONOMIC BENEFITS EXPLANATION

One of the reasons for the defence procurement mess is that, in Canada, virtually every major defence acquisition decision is not taken for military and strategic reasons, but for economic reasons. In the defence market, some buyers — that is, governments — insist that sellers not simply engage in a straight cash transaction, but accept a commitment to provide economic benefits to the purchaser in return for securing the sale. In other words, the vendor is required to "pay off" the buyer for the privilege of having secured the contract — by offsetting the price of the equipment paid to the vendor by providing economic benefits, usually equal in value to the price of the contract. The practice of requiring offsets comes from the widespread view that monies spent on a defence product should actually produce a greater return than simply the "national defence" benefit being acquired by the purchase of a particular weapons system.

Hence, many defence contracts include provisions that the vendor accept offset commitments that are explicitly designed to produce other benefits to the customer than "defence." These offsets include *co-production*, which serves to integrate firms in the buyer's economy in the global value chains of the primary producer, and *licenced production* or *sub-contractor production*, which invariably results in employment in the purchaser's economy. Other forms of offsets include placing investments in the purchaser's economy, facilitating *technology transfer*, or engaging in different forms of *countertrade*, such as barter, counter-purchase, or buy-back.[6]

Canada was one of the first countries to insist on this practice. The policy had its origins in the major procurement programs of the mid-1970s — Leopard main battle tanks, the long-range patrol aircraft, and CF-18 Hornets.[7] These offsets were formally called industrial and regional benefits (IRBs), reflecting their purpose: to generate activity in Canada's industrial base and to distribute these benefits across Canada's various regions. After the new Defence Procurement Strategy (DPS) was announced by the Harper government in February 2014, they have since been known as industrial and technological benefits (ITBs), though there is still the expectation that ITBs will be spread across Canada's regions.

The government department responsible for encouraging economic development administers defence offsets. It has had a variety of names: the Department of Industry, Trade and Commerce (IT&C), then Industry Canada, and, after the Liberal government under Justin Trudeau took office in November 2015, Innovation, Science and Economic Development Canada.

Today, Canada's ITB policy is designed to ensure that defence procurements generate "high value-added business activity for Canadian industry" equal to 100 percent of the value of the contract signed with the Canadian government. While prior to 2014 IRB offset proposals for most defence projects were judged on a pass/fail basis, the new strategy embraces a requirement that was introduced in the National Shipbuilding Procurement Strategy (NSPS), also brought in by the Harper government in 2010.[8] The NSPS not only required bidders to commit to offsets worth 100 percent of the contract price, but also required them to propose a "value proposition" equivalent to 0.5 percent of the contract price for "long-term capacity development" of "strategic partners" in the Canadian marine sector. In 2014, the same model was extended to defence projects of $100 million or more, with the requirement that bidders had to indicate how they would support "key industrial capabilities" (KICs) identified by the government. Unlike the pass/fail criteria of the IRBs, the "value propositions" were rated and weighted in bid evaluations — all in the hope that such a policy would close what a 2011 review of support for research and development, the Jenkins report, called the "procurement gap."[9]

However, as Pierre Lagueux, a former ADM (materiel) in DND, reminds us, while inserting multiple objectives in defence spending might be understandable, there is a risk of having "industrial development objectives trump the goal of acquiring the best military solution."[10] Certainly the embrace of offsets will always make procurements more expensive than a straight trans-action where a government buys a product "off the shelf" for cash, complicating the determination of what the "right price" is.

Consider, for example, the case of the production of the Iltis jeep discussed in Chapter 1: Volkswagen AG was able to produce an Iltis for $26,500; a fleet of two thousand bought off the shelf from Volkswagen would have cost the Canadian government approximately $51 million. By contrast, having Bombardier Inc. in Montreal produce them under licence cost $84,000 per unit, or approximately $168 million for the fleet. In this case, what was the right price for the Iltis jeep fleet? The question cannot be answered unless one attaches a value to the "good" of providing a flow of profitable work for Bombardier — and thereby wealth for the members of the Beaudoin-Bombardier families who control the firm, returns to the firm's other share-holders, and work (and thus wealth) for its employees. If de-fence were the *only* good being sought, then the right price for that fleet of Iltis jeeps would have been $51 million.

The willingness of governments in Ottawa to pay a premi-um to ensure that their defence spending produces non-defence benefits reflects a more widespread belief that indigenous pro-duction of a weapons system is more desirable than being de-pendent on others for supplying defence systems and buying those systems off the shelf. Not only does indigenous develop-ment and production serve the nation's defence, this argument goes, but it also strengthens the defence industrial base, and the technology developed (or transferred) also creates spin-offs that redound to the economic benefit of the country. Moreover, a weapons system that is successfully developed indigenously can be marketed and sold to the armed forces of other countries.

One can see elements of these beliefs consistently at work. At the beginning of the twentieth century, Sir Wilfrid Laurier, Sir Frederick Borden, and Sam Hughes were all moved by the idea that it was well worth the premium to manufacture rifles in Canada, particularly if it could establish Canada as a leader within the Empire for small-arms production. We can see similar sentiments at work in the middle of the century, when the St. Laurent Liberal government enthusiastically agreed to commit millions of dollars to the production of the CF-105 Arrow in an effort to make Canada a world leader in the manufacture of fighter-interceptors. And we can see elements of these beliefs at the end of the century in the willingness of Art Eggleton to interfere in the Iltis replacement so that a military vehicle that was otherwise disqualified was considered — for no other reason than it was "designed and manufactured in Canada by Canadians," and would create jobs in Canada.

In each of those cases, the decision to make defence decisions for economic and employment reasons contributed to the "messiness" of the defence procurement. Certainly the decision of the Chrétien government — and confirmed by both the Harper Conservative and Trudeau Liberal governments in the years since 2006 — to recapitalize Maritime Command (as the navy was known between 1968 and 2011) with Canadian-built ships is one of the key reasons why the Royal Canadian Navy is at present in such a crisis. While buying naval vessels "off the shelf" is highly problematic,[11] even more problematic is an approach that tries to produce highly complex naval vessels once a generation, which creates a highly dysfunctional "boom and bust" shipbuilding industry. For once a particular naval build is finished and the government stops feeding work to a shipyard, that shipyard is much more exposed to regular market forces and will shed workers — and the expertise that they have. Then, in twenty years, when the government once again wants new naval vessels, and wants to have them built in Canada, shipyards struggle to put the capacity back in place. (As we will see in the next chapter, the National Shipbuilding Procurement Strategy of 2010 was intended to put an end to this "boom and bust" approach by feeding constant work to Canada's shipyards over a thirty-year period.)

The relationship between procurement messes and the insistence that decisions on defence acquisitions be determined by economic benefits rather than defence benefits can also be illustrated by looking at one of the commonalities of the defence procurements in Canada judged to be "successful": the New Fighter Aircraft program in the late 1970s that resulted in the acquisition of CF-18s; the acquisition of the M777 howitzers in 2005–06; and the acquisition of a fleet of C-17 Globemasters by the Harper government. All of these procurements were off-the-shelf purchases. In other words, these systems were acquired by the CAF without any effort to Canadianize them or to require that the manufacturer establish a production line in Canada.

In the case of the NFA, Pierre Trudeau and his cabinet were quite clear in the ground rules they imposed on the bureaucracy to prevent the kind of gamesmanship that had been so evident in the LRPA acquisition. The winning aircraft would have to be either operational or in the advanced stages of development. The option of building the aircraft in Canada under licence to a foreign company (as the CF-5s, built by Canadair Ltd. under licence from Northrop Corporation, had been) was deemed too expensive. Moreover, there was to be no "gold-plating" — the addition of special (and thus expensive)

"Canadianized" options that might have been wanted by Air Command, as the RCAF was then known. The aircraft eventually recommended by the bureaucracy, and approved by the government of Trudeau *père*, was the McDonnell Douglas F/A-18 Hornet, a naval fighter jet. Even though Canada no longer operated an aircraft carrier, the Hornets came with all the gear necessary for carrier operations, such as folding wings, the heavier and robust landing gear needed for hard carrier landings, and arrestor hooks. But Air Command was allowed to make no "Canadianization" modifications. Only one tiny modification was permitted: the removal of the catapult attachment on the nose-wheel. A similar approach, it might be noted, was taken in the case of the M777 howitzers and the C-17 Globemasters: they were simply bought off the shelf and put immediately in service.

THE POLITICAL GAMESMANSHIP EXPLANATION

It will be quite clear, particularly from the accounts of the fiascos in the previous chapter, that one of the reasons that defence procurement is such a mess is that Canadian politicians have no hesitation in playing politics with defence procurements when it suits them.

By "playing politics," I do not mean the normal process of making policy decisions. After all, every decision made by government is always and inherently *political* — since one cannot make decisions about the authoritative allocation of a political community's treasure or its values without being political. This is particularly true of defence policy, which involves the commitment of armed forces to the defence of the community: defence decisions are always particularly political.

Rather, playing politics refers to the use of public policy issues for narrow partisan advantage to the political party "playing" with the issue. The "game" analogy is intended to underscore the essentially frivolous nature of the behaviour: instead of taking decisions for *serious reasons of national interest*, decisions are taken for reasons that are, from a national interest perspective at least, frivolous and unserious, because they are taken for the pure purpose of partisan advantage.

We can see such gamesmanship at work in a number of the procurements surveyed in the previous chapters. Certainly the Ross rifle case was riddled with political gamesmanship from the outset: the inclusion of friends of Sir Charles Ross on the committee appointed to test the weapon; the appointment of a Conservative MP, Sam Hughes, by a Liberal minister, Sir Frederick Borden, to blunt Conservative opposition to the Ross; the essentially political response by Hughes — and his prime minister, Sir Robert Borden — when the Ross began to fail Canadian troops in 1915.

So too was there considerable gamesmanship in the handling of the massive cost blow-out of the CF-105 Arrow: both the Liberals and the Progressive Conservatives played politics with the timing of what everyone in the system knew had to be the logical outcome: cancellation. The Liberals, confident that they would be re-elected, kicked the decision down the road to avoid the negative electoral consequences of a cancellation. The Conservatives, having won a minority, also deferred the decision for narrow partisan purposes — but they ended up wearing the results of the earlier Liberal games.

The gamesmanship that we see in these cases, however, pales next to the political games that were played in the Sea King replacement and the F-35 acquisition. As the accounts in the previous chapter make clear, the decision by Jean Chrétien and the Liberals to cancel the EH101 contract was made for nothing other than narrow partisan reasons. The fact that Chrétien and his front bench consistently and purposely spun the EH101 in particular ways — and refused to even mention, much less acknowledge, any of the positive benefits of the Conservative choice — demonstrates clearly what the motives at play were.

And that decision, having cost taxpayers some $500 million in wasted funds, then had to be supported with more games: the (unsuccessful) attempts to avoid having AgustaWestland win the search-and-rescue helicopter contract, or the (successful) attempts to ensure that the decision process was sufficiently torqued that the EH101 could not possibly win the maritime helicopter competition. At no point did a *strategic* or *military* consideration play a part in the evolution of the Sea King replacement between 1993 and 2004: it was all partisan politics, all the time.

A similar dynamic "explains" the F-35 fiasco. After the Conservatives came to power in 2006, the F-35 process was torqued by the Harper government for overtly partisan purposes. In particular, there was no effort to ensure that the political party that had first committed Canada to the Joint Strike Fighter program was brought along. On the contrary: the F-35 simply became part of the larger Conservative effort to bash the Liberals and help to secure Harper's self-acknowledged broader partisan political goal of having the CPC replace the Liberals as Canada's "natural governing party." And, as we saw in Chapter 2, the Liberals had no difficulty in returning the favour. Beginning in 2010, the Liberal party did all that it could to undermine the F-35, using it as a political cudgel against the Harper government. The Liberals relished the discomfort of the Conservatives as the "cost" of the F-35 climbed from $9 billion to $16 billion, and then to $29 billion, $36 billion, and finally $45 billion in the space of merely thirty months. Indeed, the Liberals pretended that these were real cost increases, rather than portraying them for what they really were: variations on an unchanging cost of the program of approximately $1 billion per year.

And the use of the F-35 in the 2015 election campaign was a bit of political gamesmanship borrowed directly from the Chrétien era. There was no *military* or *strategic* justification for declaring that Canada would not acquire the F-35 or allow Lockheed Martin to participate in the "open competition" that the Liberals were promising to launch if they were elected.

And, once again, as an indicator of the importance of this factor as an explanation for the dysfunction, it might be noted that such gamesmanship was noticeably absent from all the "successful" defence procurements. In the late 1970s, the government of Pierre Elliott Trudeau did not try to play politics with the NFA acquisition as a means of scoring points for the Liberals against the Progressive Conservatives under Joe Clark. And the PCs, for their part, did not seek to undermine the NFA process. The same was true with the M777 and C-17 Globemaster decisions, which were made in the context of Canada's mission in Afghanistan; neither the Harper government nor the opposition parties sought to use these procurements for partisan political purposes.

❖

The explanations above for the dysfunction in defence procurement in Canada are, however, only *proximate* explanations. In other words, these factors, either separately or taken together, might provide us with an explanation for the *immediate* causes of a particular dysfunction, or why a particular procurement went off the rails. We can thus point to the institutional arrangements under which defence equipment is acquired, or to the distortions created by such factors as Canadianization or the need for offsets, or the willingness of political leaders to politicize procurements. Using these factors, we can explain this or that procurement.

But what these factors do not provide is the *ultimate* explanation. Sometimes called "distal" explanations (because they are more distant from immediate causality), these factors would enable us to better explain the proximate explanations. For example, to argue that the Sea King replacement became the fiasco it did because Chrétien politicized it in 1993, and that from that point the rest of the sorry tale unfolded in a nicely path-dependent way, begs a much more important set of questions: *why* did Chrétien and the Liberal party feel so confident in being able to use the EH101 purchase as a political tool for electoral gain? *Why* was the Liberal government so utterly unconcerned about wasting $500 million in cancelling the contract? *Why* did the Chrétien government try its very hardest to torque the process so that the EH101 would not win either of the competitions (failing in the case of the search-and-rescue procurement but succeeding in the maritime helicopter case)?

To understand why Canadian defence procurement looks as it does — and thus to understand how to "fix" it — we need to examine a much broader range of causality. And the most important ultimate, or distal, explanation for the dysfunctions in Canadian procurement is, I argue, to be found in the "security imaginary" of Canadians; the immunity that Canadian politicians enjoy from electoral punishment for poor defence management; the "wide eyes" of Canadian politicians; and the fundamental contradiction that this causes.

THE CANADIAN "SECURITY IMAGINARY"

International relations scholars have a bit of jargon to capture the way in which people think about their country's location in global politics: they call it the "security imaginary."[12] Behind the jargon, however, lies an important point: the way in which people think about their country's security in the world is largely a function of *imagination*. In other words, Canadians conceive of their country's position in the world in particular ways, some of which may have nothing to do with reality. For example, Canadians overwhelming think of their country as a peace-keeping nation, even though that role is and always has been largely mythological. But that actually doesn't matter: as long as Canadians *imagine* their country as a peacekeeper, that will shape their expectations and their aspirations; that will shape what policies they will support and what policies they will oppose.

Most Canadians today have never heard of David Mills, a Liberal MP who represented the riding of Bothwell in Kent and Lambton counties in Ontario for twenty-seven years in the late nineteenth century. But the way Mills "imagined" Canadian security is how vast numbers of Canadians have conceived of defence over the years — and continue to do so to this day. Speaking to the House of Commons in 1875, Mills put it like this: "In a country situated as we are, not likely to be involved in war, and having a large demand upon our resources for public improvements, it [is] highly desirable to have our military affairs conducted as cheaply as possible."[13] In just thirty-nine words, he captured the core reasons why Canadians have the attitudes they do toward defence. Canada's location — separated from the rest of the world by three oceans, with a harshly inhospitable polar region on our northern approaches and the United States, a dominant and now hegemonic power, as our southern neighbour — means that Canadians have the extraordinary luxury of being able to devote their wealth to things other than defence, so that whatever defence needs to be done can — and should — be done on the cheap.

It is clear that successive generations of Canadians have agreed. But if Canadians are complacent about national security, neglectful of the armed forces, indifferent to military matters, and, above all, cheap and unwilling to spend on defence, it is because history has shown them that, given Canada's geostrategic location in North America, we Canadians do not *need* to take defence seriously. As Desmond Morton pointed out long ago,[14] Canada has never suffered from the indifference that Canadians have persistently exhibited to defence.

In alliances, those who do not pull their weight financially are criticized as "free riders," since they enjoy the benefits of security provided by the alliance without making an appropriate contribution to the collective. Joel Sokolsky, former principal of the Royal Military College of Canada, argues that Canadians do not completely "free ride" on others in the Atlantic alliance, but they certainly do devote as little of their considerable national wealth as possible to the armed forces. We are not so much free riders, Sokolsky argues, as "easy riders." [15] Over the years, the calculation has come down to a simple question: what is the *minimum* amount of money that we can get away with?

The results of that calculation can be seen in the yawning gap between what Canada and its allies spend on defence. In 2014, Canada devoted just 1.0 percent of gross domestic product (GDP) to defence. In the same year, only seven of the twenty-eight NATO allies spent less than Canada as a percentage of GDP. And the allies that Canada is closest to — the United States, Britain, France, and Australia — all spent much more. The United States devotes 3.3 percent of its GDP to defence; Britain, 2.0 percent; France, 1.9 percent; and Australia 1.8 percent. [16] The official NATO target, agreed to in 2014 by all allies, including Canada, is 2.0 percent.

Moreover, Canadians have demonstrated, clearly and unambiguously, that they support governments in Ottawa that seek to drive military spending in peacetime down to the lowest levels acceptable to Canada's allies. Certainly Canadian voters have not rewarded governments in power — or opposition parties vying for power — that promise to spend *more* on the military in peacetime. Consider: by 2016, Canada's spending on defence had fallen to 0.9 percent of GDP. What political party would win power in the next election by promising to spend 2.0 percent, the level of spending Canada promised in 2014? Perhaps more to the point, what political party would even *think* of promising to move to such a level in the first place?

It needs to be stressed again that this cheapness is not just a contemporary phenomenon. It is true that we can see this unwillingness of Canadians to spend on defence more clearly in the present era, after the end of the Cold War and in the aftermath of the Afghanistan mission. However, historically Canadian expenditures on defence during peacetime have always been relatively low: in the years before the First World War, in the interwar period (1919–39), and in the immediate aftermath of the Second World War. It is only during times of war — the First World War, the Second World War, the Korean War, and the Afghanistan mission — that we have seen significant spikes in spending.

What impact does this security imaginary have on defence procurement? I argue that there are two major effects. First, the security imaginary creates a highly permissive environment for Canadian politicians, since the indifference to defence issues that is engendered by the security imaginary is mirrored, paradoxically, by an indifference towards the mismanagement of defence policy. Second, it creates a fundamental contradiction in Canadian defence policy that has a very direct impact on procurement. To a consideration of these effects we now turn.

A PERMISSIVE POLITICAL ENVIRONMENT

The lack of concern about defence that comes from the security provided by Canada's geostrategic location has an important impact on defence procurement. The indifference of Canadians to defence spending extends, paradoxically, to the mismanagement of what few resources Canadians do devote to defence.

Consider the hundreds of millions of dollars that have been spent on the messes surveyed in this book. Some of the wasteful expenditures were the result of increased costs as a result of exchange rate fluctuations that occur as a result of delays in the procurement process. Some of the waste occurred because of the "cost-plus" approach to Canadian defence contracting that at least one foreign defence contractor has publicly characterized as "bizarre." Alex Vicefield, CEO of the company that owns Davie Shipyard in Quebec City, has said that in all his years in the procurement system, "never have I witnessed a country so willing to spend money unnecessarily.… It's almost as if money is no object."[17] And some expenditures did nothing more than fill the coffers of foreign defence contractors, with no "return" to Canadians at all: consider the $478.3 million quite literally thrown away by the new Chrétien government on its very first day in office in November 1993 when it decided to cancel the EH101 helicopter contract discussed in the previous chapter.

It is true that some of those expenditures produced employment for Canadians, but it is not clear that the employment was as productive as it might have been had the expenditures been made in ways that did not result in such waste. Moreover, some of the employment "benefits" have been ephemeral or subject to the arbitrary whims of governments: think of the fourteen thousand Avro employees who were fired in February 1959 because the Diefenbaker government decided to abandon the millions of dollars that had been sunk into the Arrow, or the 750 Paramax employees who were fired in November 1993 because the Chrétien government decided to play politics with the EH101, or the countless shipyard employees on the east and west coasts and at Davie in Quebec City who faced uncertain periods of employment as a result of Canada's boom-and-bust approach to naval shipbuilding.

And yet, despite the huge mismanagement of defence procurement by governments in Ottawa on both sides of politics, Canadians have persistently and unambiguously shown that they have little interest in punishing their governors for persistently getting defence procurement "wrong" or for knowingly and consciously wasting hundreds of millions of dollars.

At first blush, it may seem strange that Canadian governments routinely manage to escape electoral retribution for their mismanagement of defence policy. But electoral studies tell us that even if Canadians were angered at the way in which a particular government mismanaged defence procurement, voters generally predicate their ballot-box choices on criteria other than a single salient issue. Poor management of defence procurement has never been a central issue in any election campaign and is unlikely to become one in the future. The reason is simple: both the Liberals and the Conservatives have such an abysmal record in managing defence procurement that both major parties have for a long time lived in glass houses on this issue. The result is that neither has been willing to make defence procurement an election issue. And none of the smaller parties — the New Democratic Party, the Bloc Québécois, or the Green Party — is a keen supporter of a robust Canadian military establishment to begin with, so none of them has any interest in drawing the voters' attention to the mismanagement of military affairs by the major parties.

However, it must be admitted that these explanations do not fully account for why Canadians, who are persistently stingy when it comes to defence expenditures, are also persistently in-different when the relatively few dollars that are allocated to defence are carelessly wasted by their governors. That paradox remains to be explained.

Whatever the explanation, the consequence of the per-sistent immunity from electoral punishment for getting de-fence procurement wrong is profound. It means that both of the major parties in Canada enjoy a hugely permissive political environment for "bad" behaviour on defence procurement. Both parties know that if, for example, they play politics with defence procurement — as Jean Chrétien did in 1993, or as Stephen Harper did in 2010, or as Justin Trudeau did in 2015 — there are no negative political consequences at the ballot box. If they make defence procurement decisions for non-defence reasons, as both Liberal and Conservative gov-ernments have done throughout Canadian history, or if their lack of attention to procurement detail results in hundreds of millions of dollars being wasted through delays, there will be no consequences if things do not turn out well.

Just as importantly, there are no political rewards when governments do get defence procurement right. Whatever kudos Trudeau *père* might have gained for the successful CF-18 procurement meant little in September 1984, when the Liberals lost to the Progressive Conservatives under Brian Mulroney. Likewise, the Harper Conservative government might have managed to get C-17 Globemasters, M777 howitzers, or CH-47 Chinooks delivered on time and at the right price, but those successful procurements meant little in October 2015.

THE "BIG EYES, EMPTY POCKETS" CONTRADICTION

The second way that the unwillingness of Canadians to spend on defence creates the messes in procurement outlined in this book is that the dominant security imaginary of ordinary Canadians, when it intersects with the model of the Canadian military that ministers in cabinet have in their minds, creates a fundamental contradiction that can only result in a colossal mess.

That contradiction can be easily stated: Canadians have persistently demonstrated that they have a deep aversion to spending on defence; Canadian cabinets have as persistently refused to fashion a defence policy that even acknowledges, much less reflects, that fundamental and unalterable cheapness of Canadians. The contradiction can be put in the evocative terms used by Norrin Ripsman when he sought to characterize the Mulroney government's approach to defence policy in 1987: Mulroney's cabinet, he said, had "big eyes" but "empty pockets." In other words, the ministers were very keen to acquire a range of new military systems — most notably twelve new nuclear submarines — but discovered when it came to paying the bills for these systems that the government lacked the funds or, more accurately, lacked the will to spend the huge sums that would have been required.[18] However, the big eyes / empty pockets contradiction applies with equal power to virtually all Canadian governments since the Second World War, not just the Mulroney government.

For Canadian cabinets for at least the last sixty years have all had big eyes when it comes to the military. In other words, when cabinets have made collective decisions about what kind of military they believe to be "right" for Canada, they have invariably embraced the same, unchanging model. (I stress here that I am referring to the *collective* decisions of cabinets. I acknowledge that individual cabinet ministers have come to office with a different conception of the ideal armed forces for Canada, and perhaps even articulated that conception to their cabinet colleagues. However, when aggregated into a collective decision by the cabinet as a whole, the result has been pretty unchanging over the years.)

That "model" military consists of a highly formulaic approach to the size and capability of the Canadian Armed Forces. Cabinets have generally maintained that Canada must have a "fully integrated, flexible, multi-role, and combat-capable military," to use the words of the 2008 *Canada First Defence Strategy.* Other Canadian defence papers used different words over the years, but the essence was the same.

What has this formula meant in practice? It does not mean that the CAF must have *all* of the military capabilities that are available. For example, Canada has not had nuclear weapons in its arsenal since 1984. While the Liberal government of Lester Pearson armed the Canadian forces with nuclear weapons after it won the 1963 election, Pierre Elliott Trudeau divested those weapons in 1984. The RCAF does not operate long-range bombers, close-air support aircraft like the A-10 "Warthog" or the AH-64 Apache helicopter, or lethal drones like the Reaper or the Predator. The RCN does not operate aircraft carriers, cruisers, amphibious assault ships, or littoral combat ships. The CAF does not include formations comparable to the Royal Marines in the United Kingdom or the U.S. Marine Corps.

However, judging by their decisions over the years, cabinets have always believed that Canada should maintain a fairly full gamut of military capabilities. Thus Canada has a "blue-water navy" and a submarine fleet, and it is capable of Arctic operations in the short summer sailing season. The air force flies both fixed-wing and rotary-wing aircraft: latest-generation fighters, patrol and surveillance aircraft, airborne refuellers, heavy strategic and medium-lift aircraft, search-and-rescue helicopters, anti-submarine warfare and vertical replenishment helicopters, tactical aviation helicopters, and a range of training aircraft, including an airshow demonstration team, the Snowbirds, and, when appropriate for the mission, surveillance drones and aerostats. The army has main battle tanks and artillery, and it is able to deploy mobile combat infantry and special forces. And, to support Canadian forces abroad in expeditionary mode, the CAF has extensive logistical, communications, and command capabilities. In short, even though Canada's capabilities are far more limited than those of other powers, they are still considerable.

Canadian politicians clearly get their big eyes from the defence establishment. Canada's military officers, like all professionals, have a well-developed normative model of what an "ideal" institution for their profession should look like, and what any "self-respecting" armed force should include. It is a model shaped and influenced by myriad factors, including "best practices" in the military establishments of friends and allies with whom they share a bond of comradeship.

The big eyes of ministers in cabinet create a huge contradiction, however. One simply cannot get a first-class military with such a wide range of capabilities without spending considerably more than the 0.9 percent of GDP that is at present devoted to the defence budget. As a result, what we have seen is a persistent but entirely contradictory approach to defence policy. On the one hand, cabinets will agree — or at the very minimum choose not to openly disagree — with the professional defence establishment that Canada really should have a substantial multi-role and combat-capable military. On the other hand, those same ministers will, by their spending decisions, show that they agree with Canadians at large that defence spending should be kept low.

And so Canadian governments have embraced long cycles of boom-and-bust defence spending. Spending was dramatically ramped down after the Second World War but cranked back up in the 1950s. It declined somewhat in the 1960s and then was cut hard by Pierre Elliott Trudeau in the early 1970s. However, Trudeau then moved to re-equip the armed forces in the mid-1970s, creating an increase in defence spending in the 1980s during the Mulroney era, when the bills for those big-ticket items came due. Defence spending then began to decline slowly in the late 1980s. The decline sharply accelerated in the 1990s, as the Chrétien government used the defence budget to help get federal spending into balance after two decades of deficit spending under Trudeau *père* and Mulroney, plunging the armed forces into a so-called decade of darkness.

In 2004–05, the Martin government began to reverse course on defence spending, a course continued and then accelerated by the Harper government in its first years in power. Indeed the Conservatives promised in 2008 that they were going to put in place a scheme for "predictable funding increases over a twenty-year period." But eventually they reversed course: they walked away from the most important defence procurement, the CF-18 replacement, and ended up not spending as much as they had promised, deferring over $6 billion in defence spending. Trudeau *fils* came to power in 2015 promising to continue the Conservative commitments, but then immediately "re-profiled" $3 billion in defence dollars in his government's first budget in 2016, with the result that defence spending is down to 0.9 percent of GDP.

Defence procurement has inevitably followed this boom-and-bust approach. Because there has never been enough money to do the job properly, numerous systems have been allowed to rust out, including "little" ones like the Iltis jeeps and major ones like the *Oberon*-class submarines, the auxiliary oil replenishment vessels, and the destroyer fleet. Systems have been bought on the cheap: as we saw in Chapter 1, the *Victoria*-class submarines might have had a bargain-basement price, but the longer-term costs of actually getting and keeping them operational were considerable. Or procurement programs have been highly politicized, as the Sea King and CF-18 Hornet replacement programs were, adding to costs, delays, and diminished capabilities.

Even the money that was made available was not always spent in an efficient way. Because, as we have seen, the military tends to require that weapons systems be Canadianized, this invariably means that many systems become far more costly than they would be if they were put into use "as is." The CF-105 Arrow program in the 1950s remains the classic example of spiraling costs spent on trying to create a fighter aircraft with Canadian characteristics. But there are other more recent examples where Canadianization increased initial costs: the torpedoes on the *Victoria*-class submarines, the various modifications to the Boeing CH-147 Chinooks and the Sikorsky CH-148 Cyclones, or the prospective modification of the plans for the joint support ships.

Governments find it almost impossible to buy military equipment without insisting that such purchases produce an economic return to Canadians, either via building weapons systems in Canada or via industrial and technological benefit offsets placed in the Canadian economy. This means that Canadians routinely pay a premium to acquire particular military capacities. Although off-the-shelf purchases would generate huge savings for Canadians, recent off-the-shelf purchases have been primarily limited to emergency expenditures during the Afghanistan mission.

In other words, it is the fundamental contradiction in Canadian defence policy that is the distal cause of the messes we see: Canadians won't spend on defence, but Canadian governments refuse to cut their (military) coat according to their cloth. Instead, Canadian politicians pretend that the CAF can maintain significant capabilities while spending just 0.9 percent of GDP. Rust-out, extended lives, diminished capability, and periodic scrambles for replacement inexorably follow, exacerbated by a political culture that deems it acceptable to play politics with defence procurement.

The argument that the security imaginary that is dominant in Canadian politics simply does not "imagine" a Canada that needs a robust armed forces because the country's security is backstopped by our geostrategic location has considerable implications for defence procurement. It explains why defence budgets are as persistently low as they are in peacetime. It also explains why Canadians are generally so indifferent to the state of the armed forces — in the sense that significant numbers of Canadians do not insist that their governments tax them more robustly in order to provide up-to-date, state-of-the-art equipment for the CAF. It explains why governments have exceedingly wide room for manoeuvre in defence procurement, including making defence decisions for "non-defence" reasons. That room for manoeuvre not only explains why Canadian governments (and Canadians more generally) are so attached to the economic offset model, but it also explains why Canadian politicians will happily play games with defence procurements when they feel that such gamesmanship is in their partisan political interest.

Such an explanatory framework also has implications for how the system might be changed. In the next two chapters, we explore ways that defence procurement in Canada could be done better. We begin by looking at recent efforts to reform the system.

4

REFORMING THE SYSTEM?

I t must be admitted at the outset that there are good reasons to be skeptical that the defence procurement "mess" in Canada can be reformed. After all, as we noted in the introduction, defence procurement is one of the most complex areas of public policy, and the complexities of defence acquisition seem to bedevil governments all over the world. Moreover, governments routinely devote considerable energy to trying to improve their defence acquisition processes in an effort to get procurement right — and they seem to have relatively little success.

This has certainly been the case in the United States. For over eighty years the U.S. has operated the world's largest and most complex defence procurement system; today it spends more than $600 billion a year on defence, more than all the other major powers combined. However, even though the U.S. has spent trillions of dollars on the development and procurement of weapons systems over many decades, its defence acquisition system has always been plagued by problems of different sorts. As a result, the reform of that system has been a constant public policy goal for at least the last fifty years. Between 1960 and 2010, defence procurement reform was studied extensively in the U.S.: fully twenty-seven studies were produced by blue ribbon panels, expert commissions, Congressional committees, task forces convened by the U.S. secretary of defense, and bureaucratic agencies like the U.S. Government Accountability Office, not to mention numerous academic teams. In 2011, these studies and their conclusions were reviewed by J. Ronald Fox, a professor in the Harvard Business School who had also worked as assistant secretary of the U.S. Army in charge of procurement. Fox ruefully concluded that there had not been much progress in fifty years of attempted reform of the defence acquisition system: "Despite the many studies and the similarities of their findings, major defense programs still require more than fifteen years to deliver less capability than planned, often at two to three times the initial cost."[1]

While defence acquisition reform has been extensively studied in the United States, there has been little comparable work done in Canada on ways to improve defence procurement, even though those who have worked in the Canadian defence procurement system invariably have ideas about how the process can be improved, and even though governments have been so persistently burned by defence acquisitions gone awry.

In 2006, Alan S. Williams published a detailed critique of the defence procurement process in Canada, together with an extended set of suggestions for improvement in defence acquisition.[2] Not without reason did Williams subtitle his book *A View from the Inside*: he had been an assistant deputy minister in two departments, responsible for overseeing some $11.2 billion in acquisitions. From 1995 to 1999, he was an ADM in Public Works and Government Services Canada; from 1999 until his retirement in 2005, he was the ADM (materiel) in the Department of National Defence.

Williams proposed twenty-five recommendations for substantial changes in the way that Canada acquires defence equipment. His most important suggestion was the creation of new lines of authority for defence procurement. Instead of the shared accountability that we examined in the previous chapter, he proposed a new and separate government department, Defence Procurement Canada, with its own minister in cabinet, empowered to procure goods and services for DND. In his view, having a single department, with a single minister in cabinet responsible for defence procurement, would streamline processes, eliminate the slowness in securing approval, simplify communications, result in increased cost savings, and, most important, deliver equipment on time.

Williams also proposed a variety of other reforms, both small and large. Many of his recommendations seemed like small procedural and technical tweaks, such as his recommendation that DND be reimbursed for the additional costs of invoking 504.5(a) of the Agreement on Internal Trade (AIT) of 1995. In Williams's view, however, such tweaks were important, since the rules under which the bureaucracy plays inevitably had an important impact on behaviour — and thus policy outcomes. In this particular example, Section 504.5(a) of the AIT allowed a preference for up to 10 percent Canadian value-added in a procurement. This was an intended benefit for Canadian industry, but it was not being used, because DND routinely avoided it since it added 10 percent to the cost of the procurement. If DND were repaid that 10 percent, Williams argued that DND would be far more willing to include Canadian value-added.[3]

A more far-ranging recommendation was for DND to incorporate full life-cycle costs into all of its strategic, planning, and procurement systems. In other words, the cost of a system had to include not only the cost of the equipment itself (the "fly-away," "sail-away," or "drive-away" costs), but *all* the costs that would be incurred in operating the system from initial deployment until the final disposal of the equipment at the end of its service life. This would be a major change, because many of the weapons systems used by the CAF have life cycles of forty years, and estimating what the full range of costs will be that far into the future tends to vastly increase the total life-cycle cost of the acquisition, as we saw in Chapter 2 in the case of the F-35. Had Williams's suggestion been adopted in 2006, everyone would have been speaking the same language about costs. The Conservative government could not have played politics with numbers by pretending that Canadians would only have to pay $9 billion for the F-35; by the same token, the Liberal opposition would not have been able to play politics with the procurement in order to make the Conservatives look foolish by playing with F-35 life-cycle numbers. And Canadians would have understood all along that a fleet of F-35s would cost them around $1 billion a year from the time they were acquired until they were disposed of sometime in the 2050s.

In 2015, Michael Byers, the Canada Research Chair in Global Politics and International Law at the University of British

Columbia, published a report for the Canadian Centre for Policy Alternatives and the Rideau Institute.[4] Released just before the start of the 2015 election campaign, this report was framed as advice to the "next government," and aimed to demonstrate how a new government could reframe defence policy in the wake of what Byers called the "crisis in defence procurement" caused by the Harper government's mismanagement. While *Smart Defence* sought to take a holistic approach to surveying what the CAF might need in the years ahead to perform the missions and roles assigned to them, Byers devoted a chapter to improving defence procurement, offering twenty-three recommendations.

Like Williams, Byers focused some of his suggestions on the organizational issue, suggesting, for example, that the minister of national defence be given the sole authority for defence procurement. Byers also recommended that all defence procurements be bought strictly off the shelf, with no Canadianization allowed. He strongly recommended against sole-source contracting, and argued that industrial and technological benefits should be reconsidered, with all military equipment purchased "on the basis of straight-up, competitively determined prices." Finally, he recommended the establishment of a House of Commons Standing Committee on Defence Procurement to increase oversight capabilities.

However, the recommendations to improve defence procurement in these extended works by Williams and Byers, not to mention the proposals for reform in shorter pieces by analysts like Dave Perry, Charles Davies, or Craig Stone, have largely fallen on deaf ears in official Ottawa. It is puzzling that, although governments in Canada, both Liberal and Conservative, have been badly burned by defence procurement messes, we have seen so few efforts by the government to reform the process.

In 2003, for example, the minister of national defence, John McCallum, created an Advisory Committee on Administrative Efficiency for DND and the Canadian Forces. The committee sought to address what it regarded as a deeply entrenched "cultural aversion to programmatic risk" that created "resistance to all but the most incremental change," and recommended significant shifts in how Canada should manage procurement.[5] Ironically, the committee's primary recommendation — that a dedicated procurement group be established within DND — was not implemented because of resistance from senior officials within PWGSC opposed to losing control over the process.[6]

The Conservatives came to office in February 2006 committed to supporting the military. The Harper government was keen to continue the process, started by Paul Martin, to end the so-called decade of darkness that the CAF had endured under Jean Chrétien. However, it could not avoid the defence procurement mess. As we have seen, it inherited a number of projects that had serious problems, such as the Sea King replacement project. The joint support ship (JSS) project resulted in such high bids that the government rejected them in 2008 and decided to design a new strategic approach to the procurement of government ships.

The result was the National Shipbuilding Procurement Strategy (NSPS), announced in June 2010. This program was intended to take a very long-term view of naval and coast guard procurement for Canada. First, the strategy embraced the firm commitment that the Canadian government would not buy the ships it needed for the Royal Canadian Navy and the Canadian Coast Guard off the shelf, but would build them in Canada. Second, instead of procuring ships on a project-by-project basis, which had resulted in a boom-and-bust cycle for Canadian shipyards in the past, the government announced that it would bundle its shipbuilding needs in long-term packages and establish a strategic partnership with shipbuilders that would ensure that the shipyard that won the contract would have predictable work for several decades.

However, just two "bundles" were on offer to the Canadian shipbuilding industry, and one of the core rules was that one shipyard was not permitted to win both contracts: one would be chosen to build combat ships — the Canadian surface combatant and the Arctic/offshore patrol ships — and another yard would build the non-combat vessels — the JSS and the Coast Guard vessels. Given that at the time there were five shipyards in Canada that qualified to compete — Seaspan ULC of Vancouver, Davie Yards Inc. of Lévis, Quebec, and Irving Shipbuilding Inc. of Halifax, together with Seaway Marine in St. Catharines and Peter Kiewit Sons Co. of Marystown, Newfoundland and Labrador — the NSPS was designed to produce two winning and three losing companies, with all of the regional employment impacts associated with contracts work between $35 and $50 billion.

Because of the huge stakes involved — indeed, for some of the companies the stakes proved to be existential — it seemed like a procurement tailor-made for the kind of political interference by regional politicians that had featured so prominently in other defence procurements. However, the NSPS introduced significant changes in the decision process for the choice of the two winners.

First, and most importantly, Prime Minister Harper himself clearly indicated to his cabinet colleagues that he expected that the decision would be free of political interference, apparently insisting explicitly that he wanted the process to be "bulletproof" so that the Conservative government could not be accused of interfering with the outcome.[7]

To backstop Harper's order, a deputy ministers' governance committee was established, with a secretariat in PWGSC. Chaired by the deputy minister of public works, the committee included the deputy ministers of Finance, Fisheries and Oceans, Foreign Affairs and International Trade, Industry Canada, National Defence, the Privy Council Office, and the Treasury Board Secretariat. All these departments also contributed staff to a secretariat for the DMGC that was housed within PWGSC.

The government also made extensive use of independent third parties to assess the capacity of Canada's five shipyards to deliver over the long term. A leading global consultant to the marine industry, First Marine International of London, was hired to undertake a benchmarking exercise to identify what would be needed based on "best practices" globally. PricewaterhouseCoopers was hired to assess the financial capabilities of the competing yards. Finally, KPMG was hired to conduct a "process validation" (in other words, to assess whether the selection process that had been put in place would yield the outcome desired). In addition, a "fairness monitor" was appointed to provide reassurance that the processes were being conducted openly and transparently.

The process worked: when the government made the announcement in October 2011 that Seaspan had been awarded the $8 billion contract for non-combat vessels and Irving had been selected to receive the $25 billion contract for the combat ships, the government was widely praised for having run what the fairness monitor, Peter Woods, called "one of the most best, if not the best" competitions he had overseen.[8]

However, whether the reforms in the shipbuilding procurement process introduced by the government in 2010–11 will have longer-term results remains uncertain. The NSPS is a long-range strategy, and thus measures of its "success" will not be apparent for at least two decades. In the meantime, more short-term considerations have begun to push back against the strategy. The navy is quickly rusting out, and the pressure for speeding the delivery of ships has been ramped up. Davie, which had been excluded from the bipolar division of the NSPS spoils, was restructured under new management as Chantier Davie Canada and has begun pushing the Trudeau government to reconsider the 2011 decision to support just two shipyards. Moreover, the cost of the build continues to grow rapidly, with the result that, unless some future government is willing to pour new money into the procurement, both the RCN and the Canadian Coast Guard will be looking at much smaller fleets in the future.

Having sought to reform the shipbuilding procurement process, the Harper government also sought to apply the lessons learned from the NSPS more widely to other areas of defence procurement. It had already commissioned the Canadian Association of Defence and Security Industries (CADSI) to offer suggestions about how to maximize the "return" to Canada's defence industrial base. CADSI's report, delivered in December 2009, pulled no punches: "Canada penalizes itself as few other nations do, delaying essential military materials, adding non-value-added costs to itself and to industry, and inhibiting its industrial champions from winning business at home and abroad." It called on the Harper government to establish a defence industrial policy, improve defence procurement practices, and improve the governance of defence procurement.[9]

It took four years for the Conservative government to mull over CADSI's recommendations. Finally, in February 2014, it adopted a "new" procurement policy that it claimed was going to fix the problems in defence procurement that it had confronted over its eight years in power once and for all. The new Defence Procurement Strategy (DPS), the Harper government promised, would recalibrate industrial and regional benefits, improve delivery timelines, and streamline procurement processes.

However, like its Liberal predecessor, the Harper government just could not bring itself to rethink the governance of defence procurement. Although the 2009 CADSI report suggested creating a single ministerial "point of accountability," the furthest that the government would go was to replicate the governance model it had created for the National Shipbuilding Procurement Strategy: a Defence Procurement Secretariat, housed within PWGSC. The secretariat was intended to be the primary coordinating mechanism for the DPS and to provide what the government termed "rigorous advice" on capabilities, costs, and benefits.

Like the NSPS, the DPS also embraced third-party independent challenge and oversight mechanisms. The government announced that it would create a "Defence Analytics Institute" that would provide expert analysis and analysis to the various DPS organizations. Another independent third-party oversight mechanism was created to review — and challenge — the Statements of Requirements (SORs) drawn up by DND for all projects valued over $100 million (and selected projects under that amount). The Independent Review Panel on Defence Acquisition is a five-person committee; the first chair was Larry Murray, a former vice-chief of defence staff and deputy minister in a number of departments. The idea behind the proposal was simple: ensure that there was some countervailing weight to the opinions of DND and the CAF.[10]

But what was not widely acknowledged was that the Independent Review Panel on Defence Acquisition was in large part spurred by one of the factors we looked at in the previous chapter: the lack of trust that the Harper government had in DND and the CAF by 2014. While the Conservatives had come to power in February 2006 claiming to love the military, by 2014 they had had a serious change of heart: "Canada's Conservative government loves the idea of the military," Jeffrey Simpson of the *Globe and Mail* archly noted; "it just doesn't always like the military."[11] That the Harper Conservatives believed that mechanisms like an Independent Review Panel on Defence Acquisition were needed indicated just how sourly the Harper government viewed the upper echelons of the military and NDHQ.

Another indication of the poor standing of the military was the willingness of the Harper government in the final years of its time in office to defer billions of dollars in defence spending, moving these monies out of the five-year fiscal framework used by finance ministers into the future. For the finance minister, such a move immediately brightens the bottom line: funds earmarked for some item that will be purchased in the future are still "on the books" but do not appear in the present five-year framework, allowing a government to claim that it is still committed to an item but to look much more fiscally responsible than it actually is. In 2013 and 2014, the Conservatives moved a total of $6.7 billion in funds that were earmarked for defence procurements but could not actually be spent because of delays. In 2014, when the Conservative minister of finance, Jim Flaherty, took $3.1 billion from the defence budget and moved it to the future, he denied that he was reducing spending on the armed forces; however, he bluntly added a criticism of the failure of DND and the CAF to be able to move procurements through the system: "There is no point in having money there to spend if they can't spend it, which they can't."[12]

The willingness of the Harper Conservatives to move DND capital funds to some distant future beyond the existing fiscal framework spoke volumes about the government's Defence Procurement Strategy. While the DPS may have looked promising initially,[13] there were too many impediments to wholesale reform. Assessing the DPS in 2016, two years after the introduction of the new policy, David Perry concluded that the reform process was "officially stuck."[14] Some of the initiatives, such as the Independent Review Panel, were up and running, but others, such as the streamlining of the procurement process, were completely stalled. And some, such as the Defence Analytics Institute, are in a state of suspended animation since the change of government in November 2015.[15] As a result, the delays in the delivery of defence projects actually worsened in 2015, with delays in every single major project.

The Liberals came to power having promised during the election campaign to clean up defence procurement. "We will fix the broken procurement system," Joyce Murray, the Liberal defence critic, had written in August, "to ensure that the Canadian Armed Forces gets the right equipment to carry out the missions that they are likely to undertake, at the right price for taxpayers, while delivering important industrial re- gional benefits to provide good jobs for Canadians across the country."[16] And initially the Trudeau government did devote some thought to defence procurement. By February 2016, the prime minister had appointed an Ad Hoc Cabinet Committee on Defence Procurement, chaired by the minister of natural resources, Jim Carr, with the president of the Treasury Board, Scott Brison, as the vice-chair. Its members included the usual defence procurement triumvirate — the minister of national defence, Harjit Sajjan; the minister of innovation, science and economic development, Navdeep Bains; and the minister of public services and procurement, Judy Foote. It also included Marc Garneau, the minister of transport; Hunter Tootoo, the minister of fisheries, oceans and the Canadian Coast Guard; and Kirsty Duncan, the minister of science.

However, the Trudeau government's first budget, brought down in March 2016, indicated clearly that the Liberals had little interest in grasping the procurement nettle, at least not during the 42nd Parliament. To ensure that the deficit in its first budget could be kept under $30 billion, Bill Morneau, the finance minister, adopted Flaherty's tactic of moving defence procurement funds from the existing five-year budget window to a later budget period in order to brighten the bottom line, resulting in a projected deficit of $29.4 billion. As Morneau ex- plained, "In order to make sure that we have the funds available at the time when [the CAF] need those funds, we've re-profiled some money in the fiscal framework, which is currently in the 2015–16 to 2021 period. And we've re-profiled it to future years so that when we need the money, the money will be in the fiscal framework."[17] With the $3.716 billion "re-profiled" in 2016, there is now over $10 billion in large-scale capital national defence projects deferred beyond the present fiscal framework.

What the minister left unstated was that these re-profiled funds will reappear after the next election, due in October 2019, at precisely the same time that a future government — Liberal or Conservative — will be confronting the consequences of the large-scale deficits incurred by the Trudeau government in 2016–17 and 2017–18.

Looking at the slim results of recent Canadian efforts to find ways of improving defence procurement, one can readily conclude that reforming the defence procurement system in Canada is no easier than in other countries. Indeed, Christyn Cianfarani, president of the CADSI, would go much further. As she wisely notes, there are in fact no "silver bullets" to be had in this area of public policy: "if there were, governments would have adopted them long ago."[18] Instead, Cianfarani encourages us to stay away from trying to "fix" the defence procurement process; instead, she suggests that we try to find ways of gradually improving the system on an ongoing basis.

Cianfarani is right to warn us about the futility of looking for silver bullets. The defence procurement process, in Canada as in other countries, seems stubbornly resistant to reform. As a policy area, defence procurement seems prone to a fundamental messiness, as we defined that word in the introduction — in other words, a "system of problems that causes dissatisfaction." Moreover, the fact that so many of Canada's close allies — including Australia, Britain, and the United States — experience difficulties of their own in defence procurement adds weight to Cianfarani's observation.

Thus, focusing on the process may not yield solutions to the messiness that seems inherent to defence procurement. For even if the bureaucratic process ran well, it is not clear that the deeply structural problems that have afflicted Canadian defence procurement over the years would magically disappear. Indeed, that is the primary lesson of the Harper government's National Shipbuilding Procurement Strategy: just because one gets the *process* right, which the Harper government unambiguously did, does not mean that one is going to actually get the right equipment, at the right price, or at the right time. Rather, the analysis of the causes of the problems in Canadian defence procurement in the previous chapter suggests that we should focus on factors other than the organizational, technical, and operational elements of the defence procurement process itself.

That is why I argue that we need to focus on the *broader political environment* in which defence procurement occurs rather than on the *decision-making process*, for it is in that environment, as I argued in the previous chapter, that we find the causes of the particular messiness of Canadian defence acquisition. To be sure, we cannot truly fix that environment — by their nature, political environments cannot easily be changed — but by proposing changes in how we frame defence procurement within that political environment, we can reduce some of the propensity for messes, even if we cannot eliminate the problems that seem so deeply engrained in the defence procurement process. In the next chapter I propose suggestions for more effective "mess management" in Canadian defence procurement.

5

FIXING DEFENCE PROCUREMENT
IN CANADA

The purpose of this chapter is to propose ways that the Canadian government could begin to get defence procurement right. I begin with the assumption that the kind of tweaks to the system surveyed in the previous chapter will not resolve the basic problems of the defence procurement system revealed by the analysis in Chapter 3. Instead, we need to look at the broad political environment and consider how Canadian defence procurement might be improved by changing the way that ministers in cabinet — the *principals* in defence procurement — actually work. Their *agents* — the bureaucrats — are not unimportant, but it is the principals who drive the system.

My proposals are driven by the analysis in Chapter 3 that argued that there were three key distal explanations for Canada's defence procurement messes. First, Canadians have always sought to spend as little as they can get away with on defence, an aversion to spending on defence in peacetime that they come by honestly, given Canada's strategic location. Second, politicians in Canada enjoy a hugely permissive environment to get defence procurement wrong, and they face very few incentives to get procurement right. Third, governments in Canada have a normative model of the ideal military — a model that they have been persuaded by the defence establishment in Canada to embrace — that is, bluntly put, not possible to sustain given the "easy-riding" proclivities of Canadians.

My suggestions come in the form of three admonitions for those at present responsible for making defence policy — and those in opposition who aspire to form government in Canada.

CRAFT A DEFENCE POLICY FOR "EASY RIDERS"

I have argued that the principal reason that defence procurement in Canada is such a mess is that elected officials have generally not been willing or able to resolve the core contradiction in Canadian defence policy: Canadians have demonstrated quite consistently over many decades that they are profoundly unwilling to spend on defence; politicians and their "big eyes" have demonstrated over as many decades an equally consistent refusal to craft a defence policy for the country that reflects that unwillingness of the Canadian body politic to devote treasure to national defence.

Some would say that the way to resolve this contradiction would be to come up with a compelling set of reasons why Canadians should abandon their easy-riding ways and step up and support the creation and maintenance of a robust, muscular, multi-role, combat-capable, and well-equipped military. These reasons should encourage Canadians to devote appropriate resources to the acquisition and sustainment of state-of-the-art equipment instead of constantly trying to do defence on the cheap in the traditional Canadian way. In this view, Canadians should be reminded that all of our close allies spend more than Canada on defence. Indeed, if Canadians today were willing to spend an amount comparable to that spent by Australians (or indeed spend what Canadians used to spend during the governments of Pierre Trudeau and Brian Mulroney, between 1.4 percent and 1.9 percent), the defence budget would jump from its present level of $18 billion (0.09 percent of GDP) to $34–$36 billion (1.8 percent).

There is little doubt that if Canadian defence spending suddenly rose to the levels of other allies (or even returned to Cold War levels), many of the procurement problems surveyed in this book could be largely made to disappear, since the government would be able to secure much of the equipment needed for the CAF straight off the shelf. Even the Royal Canadian Navy, which needs surface combatants, could consider purchasing off-the-shelf vessels while waiting for the ships presently being built by Irving and Seaspan to flow to them between now and the early 2040s. Instead of spending money for an expensive life-extension for the *Victoria*-class submarines, the RCN could return these subs to the saline mothballs from whence they came and buy a new fleet of twenty-first-century subs. It could also purchase one or more naval ice-breakers off the shelf, giving it the capability to expand the length of its Arctic operating season. The RCAF could make do with an interim fleet of Boeing Super Hornets that the Liberal government of Justin Trudeau was thinking of purchasing in 2016, while remaining part of the Joint Strike Fighter global partnership to ensure that Canadian firms benefit from being in the Lockheed Martin F-35 global value chains, and just wait for the day when Canadians wake up to the fact that the F-35 will be the only fighter the U.S. Air Force will be flying in the 2020s and beyond. The Canadian Army could add a close combat vehicle and an up-armoured Humvee to its inventory, providing infantry sent on expeditionary missions with added flexibility and protection.

But this is Lotto 6/49 "imagine the freedom" dreaming. The very size of the budget number that would be necessary for Canadians to spend on defence like Australians — $36 billion — reveals why this simply will not happen. With the Liberal government of Justin Trudeau having embraced a budget deficit of close to $30 billion in 2016, and another multi-billion dollar deficit scheduled for 2017–18, any future government in Ottawa wanting to find an additional $18 billion for the armed forces would have to dramatically raise taxes or reduce other spending (or a combination of both). To be sure, any government in Ottawa that wanted to find such a sum could readily do it by just turning to the Goods and Services Tax (GST): after all, with each percentage point of the GST worth approximately $7 billion, the government could simply raise the additional funds needed by hiking the GST from its present level of 5 percent to 8 percent, which is just one point higher than it was when the tax was introduced on January 1, 1991. Not only would it solve the CAF's funding shortfall in a stroke, but it would also undo all the fiscal damage that virtually every economist asserts was done by the short-sighted and politicized move of the Harper Conservative government to cut the GST back to 5 percent for nothing more than parochial electoral reasons.

But what kind of compelling justification would any political party offer Canadians for such moves? More to the point: what party would even *want* to try? The only circumstance that would compel Canadians to contemplate such changes is if the geostrategic ground shifted substantially and Canada were to be involved once again in a major war. This is certainly what happened in the cases of the Korean War in 1950 and the Afghanistan mission after the deployment of a battle group to Kandahar in 2005. After Canada committed forces to the Korean War, defence spending sky-rocketed, from less than 2 percent of GDP in the late 1940s to a high of 8 percent by 1952. In 2006 and 2007, the Harper government responded to the deteriorating military situation on the ground in Kandahar province with a significant increase in funding and a number of quick off-the-shelf procurements. In neither case was there any serious political opposition to such moves. But absent such a dramatic change in Canada's geostrategic circumstances, there simply is no way to resolve the contradiction by trying to convince Canadians to give up their easy-riding ways.

A more apt way to resolve the contradiction is to be found in another lottery tag line: "Know your limit, play within it." In other words: if Canadians are not willing to fund a multi-role, combat-capable, full-spectrum military equipped with state-of-the-art systems in times of peace — and I would submit that they are not — then the only other logical way out of the contradiction is to adopt a defence policy that does not require that level of spending. In other words, determine what Canada absolutely *has* to do in defence policy and then shape the residual missions in such a way that what is left is still world-class and state-of-the-art.

Determining what Canadians absolutely have to do in defence policy is an easy task. There is only one imperative, and that has not changed since the so-called Kingston Dispensation of August

1938, when the U.S. president, Franklin Delano Roosevelt, and the prime minister, W.L. Mackenzie King, exchanged a set of mutual undertakings that continue to order North American security to this day. While receiving an honorary degree at Queen's University on August 18, Roosevelt referred to the gathering storm in European politics and declared that "I give to you assurance that the people of the United States will not stand idly by if domination of Canadian soil is threatened by any other Empire." Two days later, King reciprocated: "We, too, have our obligations as a good friendly neighbour," promising that Canada would do what was necessary to ensure that the United States would not be threatened by "enemy forces."[1] Two years later, following the fall of France, the two leaders met in Ogdensburg and declared that North American security was indivisible.

That indivisibility has persisted over the years, and it continues to this very day. In the 1940s, the U.S. government sought to ensure that its northern approaches were appropriately defended against the possibility of incursion by intercontinental bombers from the Soviet Union. In the 1950s, Canadians willingly cooperated with the United States, transforming the entire continent north of the Rio Grande into a single air defence zone and continentalizing air defence in a single joint command, the North American Air Defense Command (in 1981 renamed the North American Aerospace Defense Command). In the 1960s, intercontinental ballistic missiles replaced manned bombers as the primary threat posed by the Soviet Union. In 1991, the Soviet Union itself disappeared, and the Cold War that had given rise to NORAD came to an end. For all the changes, however, the United States continues to regard the ability to intercept aircraft heading into North American airspace as a priority. Likewise, it continues to see the effective patrol of the maritime approaches to North America as crucial to its security.

This imperative has clear force structure implications for Canadians. The U.S. government continues to expect Canada to contribute to NORAD by deploying capable supersonic intercep-tors — in other words, fighters that meet the strategic require-ments of the U.S. Air Force for the defence of North America. Given this, Canadians do not have a lot of viable options. Certainly Canada could not make the choice that New Zealand did in 2001, at least not without incurring significant costs. In that year, the Labour prime minister, Helen Clark, decommissioned and mothballed the A4 Skyhawks flown by the Royal New Zealand Air Force (RNZAF); today the RNZAF only flies a limited num-ber of fixed-wing aircraft: P3 Orion maritime patrol aircraft for anti-submarine warfare, anti-surface unit warfare, surveillance, reconnaissance, and search and rescue; transport aircraft; and trainers. To be sure, Canadians could get out of the fighter aircraft business if they really wanted. But if Canada decommissioned its fleet of aging CF-18 Hornets and chose not to replace them, Canadians would pay a significant price in national sovereignty.

As Nils Ørvik noted many years ago, Canada has always pursued a strategy of "defence against help" in North America.[2] In other words, one of the reasons that Canadians provide secur-ity for North America is so that Canada can retain control of Canadian territory. If Canada were to withdraw from the conti-nental defence arrangement, either by decommissioning its fight-er fleet altogether or by deploying a less-than-capable fighter, the U.S. armed forces would simply step in and "help" provide se-curity for the American homeland — whether Canadians want-ed such help or not. In the absence of a Canadian fighter fleet, or if the fighters acquired by Canada were judged by the U.S. to be less than capable, the USAF would conduct patrols and interception operations in Canadian airspace, with or without Canadian permission. American forces would continue to maintain the North Warning System (NWS), the string of long-range and short-range radar stations strung along the mainland littoral from Cape Lisburne in western Alaska, across the north, and down the eastern edge of Baffin Island and the Labrador coast, all the way to Cartwright in Newfoundland and Labrador. They would maintain the operation of those installations on Canadian soil, again without Canadian permission if necessary.

Now it is highly unlikely that Canada would ever decommission its fighter fleet, for most Canadians actively support a continentalized approach to North American security for reasons other than a prudence driven by *realpolitik* and "defence against help." But does Canada's obligation to help defend the American homeland demand that Canada purchase a particular kind of fighter? If the Trudeau government chooses Super Hornets, it will provide a useful test of the "defence against help" dynamic. As the USAF begins to replace its F-15 and F-16 fighters currently assigned to NORAD and to deploy its fifth-generation stealthy F-35s to join its stealthy F-22 Raptors in the defence of the continental United States, will the U.S. government judge that Canada's 4.5-generation Super Hornets have the capabilities necessary for the defence of the American homeland? Some have argued that the United States will insist that Canadian non-stealthy fighters remain in the background while Canadian airspace is patrolled by stealthy American F-35s, just as Ørvik predicted in the early 1970s.[3]

Beyond the obligation to assist in the defence of the American homeland by maintaining a fighter interceptor capability and a capacity for maritime surveillance and interdiction, any other defence policy missions that one might consider all have completely discretionary implications for Canadian defence procurement.

For example, since 1949, Canada has been a party to a multinational alliance, the North Atlantic Treaty Organization, and is committed to assist in the defence of all members of the treaty if they are attacked. But precisely how that assistance is rendered is actually entirely discretionary, and thus what weapons systems might be needed to fulfill that obligation is open to discussion with Canada's NATO allies. Over the last sixty-five years, Canada's contribution to the alliance has varied. In the 1960s, large numbers of Canadian troops were stationed in Europe as part of the deterrent "tripwire" against the Soviet Union, and Canadian CF-104 Starfighter strike aircraft, armed with nuclear weapons, played a role in nuclear deterrence; today, CF-18s operate assurance missions as part of NATO's deterrent against the Russian Federation. But there is nothing deterministic about what Canada's contribution to NATO might look like: it could take a wide variety of forms.

Likewise, since 1950, Canada has committed troops to peace operations of various kinds, but that commitment does not impose particular requirements on what kind of force structure is needed. Because Canada never engages in expeditionary operations unilaterally, but always in coalitions with other partners, it can always choose to offer whatever is most useful to the coalition. Canada could, if it wished, choose to specialize in any number of areas — any, or all, would make some useful contribution.

The CAF contributes to disaster relief, but that relief could be delivered in a variety of ways and certainly structured differently than the Disaster Assistance Response Team (DART) is structured at present. For example, the government could mandate that the CAF operate a floating hospital ship to deliver disaster relief rather than, or in addition to, the present array of equipment.

In short, having a variety of defence missions that all have discretionary options for force structure opens a wide gate for Canadian defence procurement possibilities because, apart from what is needed for North American aerospace and maritime defence, no capability is *absolutely* required. Unlike most political communities in the international system, Canadians are in the exceedingly luxurious position of being able to choose what capabilities they want to have.

To be sure, actually making the move from the present multi-role force structure to a more selective military force would not be at all easy. Shortly after he was sworn in as prime minister, Justin Trudeau promised that his government would "reinvest in Canada's military, making it stronger and leaner, more agile, and better equipped."[4] His government's efforts in 2016 to make good on that promise demonstrate how difficult it is to actually make those choices.

The process of choosing which capabilities to spend on will always be highly contentious, for there will always be those who will argue that anything less than a "multi-role" armed forces would be problematic. One cannot have a *real* military, some would say, without this or that capability (or, more commonly, *all* capabilities); others would sneer that a serious country in world affairs needs a full array of hard-power capabilities. The various "tribes" that comprise the armed forces would argue that their particular specialty should of course be continued, mostly on prudential grounds: it makes sense to maintain a full range of military capabilities, it will be said, "because you never know when you will need [insert name of military "tribe" here] to fight the next war."

These are not spurious arguments. But the reality is that, in peacetime, Canada is not a "serious country" in global military affairs; only in times of systemic war have Canadians demonstrated a serious willingness — and a capacity — to devote considerable blood and treasure to conflicts they have judged worth fighting. In peacetime, Canadians, or so it would appear from their behaviour, have long made their peace with being a marginal player militarily.

More importantly, it can be argued that a smaller, more specialized CAF, with niche capabilities that are carefully nurtured and maintained so that they are always state-of-the-art and world-class, is actually a far better military to have than one that, while it might be larger and more multi-role, is actually in a constant state of ramshackle disarray because Canadian politicians have never really been able to reconcile their own big eyes with the empty pockets that their perpetually stingy constituents insist on.

The prudential "tribal" argument is not wrong, but it is misplaced. It is true that one really doesn't know what "future shock" in global politics will result in Canadians being at war again or what form that war will take. However, we can be almost 100 percent certain that if Canada is at war, it will never be at war *by itself,* but will always be at war alongside others in a multilateral coalition. Thus *Canada* will in fact never need [insert name of military "tribe" here], since others in the coalitions to which Canada will always belong will inevitably have that specialty. Those coalition partners whose armed forces lack a full spectrum of military capabilities are no less useful to the coalition's operations, however; they just need to ensure that they do not commit their armed forces to a mission they are ill-equipped to carry out.

THINK STRATEGICALLY, PROCURE STRATEGICALLY

In an ideal world, a country's defence procurement should flow from its defence policy. And in an ideal world, defence policy should flow from a careful examination of the country's geostrategic location, looking at both the immediate neighbourhood and the world at large. Threats to the political community and its well-being, as well as the potential damage that others in the international system might do to the nation's interests both in the short term and the longer term, are assessed. Then, on the basis of that strategic threat assessment, the government decides what is needed to keep the country "safe" against threats to the well-being and physical security of the country and its citizens. The time horizon of such calculations must be both short term and long term, and the assessment must have the resilience to be able to take account of the kind of unforeseen shocks that tend to mark global politics.

It is only when these decisions have been made that a government can decide how to organize itself: what "force structure" is likely to be required — in other words, how the armed forces are organized and equipped and, in particular, what equipment will likely be needed to defend effectively against threats; and, just as importantly, what resources will be needed to purchase, maintain, and eventually upgrade, renew, or replace this equipment. In short, defence procurement should flow from a set of prior decisions about force structure, which in turn flow from decisions about threat assessment.

As long as this process is followed, it is not necessary to articulate these various levels of defence decisions publicly. However, many governments do seek to formalize their defence policy into public documents, commonly known as strategic reviews or defence white papers. Indeed, many governments produce defence white papers at regular intervals in order to keep the analysis up-to-date in a changing world.

Articulating defence policy in a formal way has numerous political purposes — and benefits. Defence white papers signal intent to friends and allies and, importantly, to actual or possible enemies. For the government that writes the defence white paper, it can provide an internally consistent set of benchmarks for assessing policy performance, including budgetary expenditures. Finally, and most importantly, defence white papers provide a way for a government to explain to its own citizens its thinking on geostrategic issues, and thereby offer reasoned justifications for the often very expensive decisions on force structure that may flow from its geostrategic assessments.

This brief excursus into the theory of defence policymaking reminds us just how far from the norm Canadian defence policy has been, for formal articulations of Canadian defence policy are exceedingly rare. In the seventy years since the end of the Second World War, Canadian governments have issued just seven white papers or reviews of defence policy: in 1964, 1971, 1987, 1994, 2005, 2008, and the one launched in 2016.

Not one of these seven papers, however, was driven by a desire to periodically update the basic strategic decisions that are, in theory at least, supposed to drive defence policy and defence procurement. On the contrary: the dates reveal the common reason behind defence papers in Canada. Each was written by a new prime minister eager to distinguish his government's defence policies from those of his predecessor. Thus the 1964 paper was written by the Liberal government of Lester Pearson (1963–68) following the defence policy disasters of the Progressive Conservative government of John Diefenbaker (1957–63). The 1971 defence white paper sought to capture the changes that Pierre Elliott Trudeau (1968–79, 1980–84) wanted to introduce to differentiate himself from Pearson. In 1987, Brian Mulroney, the Progressive Conservative prime minister from 1984 to 1993, articulated a defence policy designed to distinguish PC defence policy from that of the Trudeau Liberals. In 1994, the Liberals under Jean Chrétien (1993–2003) issued a new defence policy to mark the transition from the Mulroney era. Like Trudeau in 1971, Paul Martin (2003–06) issued a white paper in 2005 that sought to distance Martin from his predecessor, in this case Jean Chrétien. In 2008, the Conservative government of Stephen Harper (2006–15) published the *Canada First Defence Strategy*, seeking to differentiate the Conservatives from both the Chrétien and the Martin Liberals. And finally, the defence review initiated in 2016 was an attempt by the new Liberal government under Justin Trudeau to mark a departure from the Harper years.

But the clear pattern here also reveals the fundamental flaw in Canadian practice. Defence papers in Canada are designed not as *geostrategic* exercises but as *domestic political* exercises. They have only one primary purpose and that is to show just how different the new prime minister's government is from the previous government. That means that Canadian defence papers must always be torqued to find something "new" to say about defence policy. The status quo won't do — because, after all, the very purpose of the new defence paper is to articulate a new approach.

Moreover, the fact that many years can go by without a formal statement on defence policy means that Canadian cabinet ministers routinely approve the expenditure of billions of dollars each year on maintaining a defence establishment, but only on very rare occasions do they go through the exercise of actually articulating for themselves, for Canadians more generally, and for others in the international system exactly why Canada spends what it does on defence or why the Canadian Armed Forces are equipped as they are.

It is true that the defence establishment itself — the Department of National Defence and the Canadian Armed Forces — does engage in geostrategic planning. The chief of force development in the CAF publishes an extensive and carefully documented assessment that seeks to project defence needs twenty-five years into the future. These are substantial studies: the 2014 iteration ran to 182 pages and drew on a wide range of published and unpublished sources.[5]

However, strategic planning documents like *The Future Security Environment* do not necessarily reflect the views of ministers in cabinet. Rather, they are written by military officers and bureaucrats in National Defence Headquarters and thus reflect very particular, and narrow, perspectives. In the first instance, papers like this are the collective expression of a professional *Weltanschauung*. The German word, usually translated as "a concept of the world," captures more clearly than the English "world view" the holistic nature of the process of *conceiving of the world both as it is and as it should be.* Those in the profession of arms, like all professionals, have world views that are very particular to their profession. Their world view will also profoundly shape the "security imaginary" — discussed in Chapter 3 — of those in the defence establishment. But we should not forget that such professional perspectives will also inevitably reflect the interests of the organizations of which they are a part — the CAF and DND.

By contrast, the politicians in cabinet who make the authoritative decisions about Canada's defence policy and its force structure are self-acknowledged amateurs in military affairs. It is extremely rare for anyone who has served in the CAF to be appointed as a federal cabinet minister in Canada: of the 199 individuals named to cabinet positions by six prime ministers between September 1984 and November 2015, just four had served in the armed forces. However, while they may not be well-schooled in international or strategic affairs, every minister will inevitably bring to the cabinet table their own *Weltanshauung* and their own security imaginary, based on their particular knowledge, expertise, and life experiences.

Moreover, the vast majority of cabinet ministers, not being military professionals, have little real commitment to ensuring that the CAF has the kind of state-of-the-art, world-class equipment that the military believes it needs to do its job properly. It is true that Canadian politicians will always use phrases like "state-of-the-art" and "first-class" and "modern" whenever they *talk* about equipment for what they invariably refer to as "our brave men and women in uniform." The 2008 Conservative defence white paper, for example, used the phrase "first-class, modern military" to describe the CAF fully six times and "state-of-the-art military" three times. The problem is that there has traditionally been a general unwillingness to back up the fine phrases that roll so effortlessly off the tongues of ministerial speech writers with hard cash. Instead, Canadian politicians, like the people who elect them, are quite comfortable with doing defence on the cheap.

That is why there tends to be such a huge disconnect between the defence establishment view of defence policy, on the one hand, and what a cabinet would likely write if it were required to articulate its own autonomous paper on defence policy. Unfortunately, because cabinets tend not to write their own defence papers, these papers tend to reflect the perspective of the professionals in the defence establishment.

And therein lies the problem: even though every minister brings to the cabinet table a particular security imaginary, there is a natural and quite understandable tendency to defer to the views of the professionals in the defence establishment. But there is a significant downside to such deference.

If cabinet ministers simply allow themselves to become "toothless tigers who gum the policy proposals of the senior bureaucracy,"[6] to use the memorable words of Douglas Hartle, a former deputy secretary in the Treasury Board Secretariat, the results will surely end up distorting defence policy — unless there just happens to be an exact coincidence between the policy proposals of the professional military establishment and the security imaginary of ministers in cabinet — an exceedingly unlikely prospect.

If cabinet ministers just accept without question the drafts fed up to them by NDHQ, the much likelier scenario is that cabinet will eventually discover — usually when funds have to be approved for defence procurement — that their own view of the world simply does not accord with the document that they had approved "on the nod." In that case, ministers will have no difficulty in abandoning whatever commitments had been laid out in the defence paper that they may have approved merely months beforehand.

That is exactly what happened in the cases of both the 1987 and the 2008 defence papers. In 1987, Perrin Beatty, the minister of national defence in the Mulroney government, took the draft produced for him by NDHQ that outlined a large increase in defence spending and brought it to cabinet, where it was endorsed without much discussion. When the spending implications of that white paper became fully apparent, however, ministers quickly backed away, and many of the commitments embraced in the white paper were abandoned.[7]

In 2008, the Harper Conservative government accepted the draft of the *Canada First Defence Strategy* put up to it by NDHQ. Although this document was little more than a long shopping list of new equipment wanted by the military, it was approved by cabinet without much apparent concern for the spending implications. But, as in the case of the 1987 paper, when it came time to actually spend, the Harper government backed off. The consequence was that most of the projects promised in 2008 are nowhere close to fruition, resulting in both added costs to the taxpayer and diminished capabilities for the CAF.

That is why a defence paper needs to reflect the collective security imaginary of the ministers in cabinet, not that of the professional defence establishment. In framing defence policy, NDHQ will be an important voice advising the ministers in cabinet. But it should be only one of many. The defence bureaucracy can advise; it can even prepare a first draft of what it would like to see as Canada's defence policy. But cabinet needs to *own* the defence policy that is eventually published in its name.

It is true that when ministers bring their particular world views to the table and have these views collectively expressed, the result may be a very different defence policy, and a very different force structure, than the ones preferred by the professional military and the defence establishment. But it will be a defence policy that more closely reflects Canadian political reality and will thus likely be more immunized against cabinet defection later on.

In short, to get defence procurement right, cabinets need to change the way they make defence policy. First, they need to take the formal articulation of policy much more seriously than they have in the past. While they do not need to do this in the form of a defence white paper, such documents have been best practice among Canada's allies, and, moreover, there are good domestic political reasons to formalize thinking in this way.

Second, cabinets need to write these papers for the right reasons. Why put out defence white papers at the beginning of a ministry for narrow partisan political reasons — to help establish that the new ministry's defence policy is different from that of its predecessor — when such documents are just put on a shelf and forgotten about? Instead, if cabinets began to write defence papers for geostrategic reasons, these documents would actually have ongoing value in helping guide a government to clearer defence policymaking. Laying out defence policy would help determine what the CAF will likely be required to do; that, in turn, will determine what equipment will be needed in order for it to fulfill its missions successfully; and that, finally, would determine the resources needed to pursue the policy.

Finally, Canadian defence white papers need to be written more frequently, so that a proper feedback loop can be developed in order to ensure that governments can make appropriate adjustments in policy, force structure, and procurement if necessary. Many of Canada's allies, big and small, do this already: the United States, Britain, France, and Australia all examine their defence policies at the highest level on a regular basis.[8] And while it has been argued that there are pitfalls in regular reviews that end up simply affirming what has been said in the last review,[9] it can also be argued that such problems are outweighed by positive results of being able to formally reassess policy once every several years.

Thus, as a first step toward this goal, the defence review initiated in 2016 by Harjit Sajjan, Trudeau's minister of national defence, should be taken and used as the basis for a proper full defence white paper, which would then be subjected to a regular and ongoing review. The re-articulation of Canadian defence policy in white paper form would allow the Trudeau government, and governments in the future, to begin to make serious strategic decisions to reconcile the contradictions, and these strategic decisions will, in turn, help determine defence procurement.

DON'T PLAY POLITICS WITH PROCUREMENT

Just as ministers in cabinet should not depend purely on the defence establishment for its advice on the broad shaping of defence policy, so too should they not listen only to voices from their own party when writing defence white papers. There is a good case for ensuring that defence policy — and the procurement that flows from it — becomes a more bipartisan exercise.

We usually associate bipartisanship in foreign and defence policy with the United States, where tradition has it that politics is supposed to "stop at the water's edge." In a Westminster parliamentary system, bipartisanship is made difficult by the structures of the political system. In a parliamentary system, the Official Opposition is supposed to oppose. It is supposed to find fault with the government of the day, and to present itself to the voters as a viable alternative at the next election.

Moreover, in the two-party system in the United States, we can meaningfully talk about *bi*partisanship. In Canada, where since 1921 there have always been more than two parties represented in the House of Commons, bipartisanship seems like an ill-fitting concept for what has been described as Canada's "two-and-a-half party" system.[10]

However, while the idea of bipartisanship may sit uncomfortably in a Canadian context, there once was a time when Canada's two major parties — the Liberals and the Progressive Conservatives (PCs) — did share a common view of the world, of the threats posed to Canadian interests, and of the defence policies that were appropriate to meet those threats. During the Cold War in particular, these two parties had essentially similar approaches to the main geostrategic challenges that Canada faced, and thus considerable bipartisanship on defence policy.

During this period, the approach to defence policy was literally *bi*partisan: only the two larger parties had a fundamentally shared view of the world and Canada's place in it. Of the smaller parties in Parliament during this era, only the New Democratic Party (NDP) had a clearly defined defence policy, and it evinced a very different strategic perspective that placed it well outside the bipartisan consensus: the NDP advocated a neutralist course for Canada, a withdrawal from both NORAD and NATO, and was basically unsympathetic to the use of force as a tool of Canadian statecraft.

The bipartisan consensus between the Liberals and the Progressive Conservatives basically fell apart with the end of the Cold War in the early 1990s, though that was not the cause. Rather, the end of the Cold War just happened to coincide with the severe fracturing of the Canadian party system that manifested itself so clearly in the 1993 election. The PCs were reduced to just two seats and the country was divided regionally: the separatist Bloc Québécois (BQ) swept Quebec and formed the Official Opposition; the Reform party dominated the West; the Liberals under Jean Chrétien formed a majority government based on near-complete sweeps in Ontario and the Maritime provinces.

That fracturing had a deep impact on defence policy. The BQ was committed to the dismantling of Canada and showed little interest in defence. MPs from Reform and its successor party, the Canadian Alliance, came to Ottawa with a distinctly isolationist bent. The governing Liberals were deeply divided between those MPs who wanted to pursue a traditional defence policy of strong alignment with the United States and those who saw the end of the Cold War as an opportunity to forge a more independent defence policy for Canada, with the result that there were now considerable similarities between some Liberal MPs and the NDP.

Moreover, that fracturing persisted, even after the "unite the right" movement resulted in the unification of the PCs and the Canadian Alliance in the Conservative Party of Canada in 2003 and the victory of the Conservatives under Stephen Harper in 2006. While there have been some instances of agreement between the political parties on defence issues — on the bombing of Libya in 2011, for example — there have been more areas of disagreement than areas of agreement.

However, as we have seen, the collapse of the Cold War bipartisanship had a huge — and largely negative — impact on defence procurement. The willingness of both the major parties to openly play politics with defence procurement since 1993 has wasted hundreds of millions of dollars and severely affected Canada's defence capabilities.

The analysis in Chapter 3 suggests that one way to eliminate some of the dysfunction in Canada's defence procurement system would be to try to re-establish some of the bipartisanship that we saw during the Cold War. In other words, the two major parties — the Liberals and the Conservatives — would agree to forego the short-term benefits of playing politics with defence procurements and instead cooperate with one another in trying to fashion an approach to defence policy that was as bipartisan as possible.

It should be stressed that such efforts should be *bi*partisan, not multipartisan. Neither the NDP nor the Green party has ever been able to articulate a serious defence policy, and, absent some collective eureka moment, neither is likely to develop one in the foreseeable future. And the BQ, even though it does have a much clearer approach to defence policy than the other small parties, nonetheless cannot be allowed to play any role in the formation of defence policy because the party's political goals are so deeply antithetical to the creation of a defence policy for *Canada*. Rather, the proposal here is for Liberals and Conservatives to try to forge a *bi*partisan approach to defence policy and defence procurement with each other, recognizing that the NDP and the Greens will be unlikely to support the kind of defence policy that they embrace.

The proposal for greater bipartisanship in defence policy may at first blush seem entirely counterintuitive. Why would either of the two main political parties agree to stop playing politics with defence procurement when they have the chance to score points against their opponents and increase their likelihood of electoral success — and, moreover, when there are never any costs to be paid for such behaviour?

There actually is a good reason for foregoing the short-term benefits of playing politics with defence procurement: self-interest. Defence is one policy area where the decisions taken during one parliament will generally not have consequences until much later, and certainly well past the next election. Because neither the governing party nor the main opposition party knows which one will be wearing today's defence procurement decisions in the future, each should, if they were rational, share a deep self-interest in being able to give as much bipartisan shape to these procurements as possible.

Inheritance is deeply embedded in defence procurement. In the 1980s, the Mulroney government inherited the consequences of a massive re-equipment program undertaken by Trudeau *père* in the late 1970s. The Harper government inherited two problematic procurements from the Chrétien government — the *Victoria*-class submarines and the Sea King replacement. Trudeau *fils* inherited not only the CF-18 replacement program, but also the Sea King program that had begun during his father's time in power.

Moreover, once the original set of decisions has been made, the trajectory of procurements tends to become heavily path-dependent. In other words, the costs of altering course quickly become so high that one is quite literally stuck with the inertial consequences of a previous government's decisions. Consider how the Trudeau Liberal government came to office in 2015 having to deal with not only the defence procurement messes created by their own decision to play politics with procurement while in opposition, but also the messes bequeathed them by previous governments — not just by the Harper Conservatives, but even by the Chrétien Liberals from the 1990s.

How might a government in power seek to maximize the bipartisan involvement of the other party in the shaping of defence policy? The most effective way is the approach adopted by the Progressive Conservative government of Brian Mulroney in the mid-1980s. In an unprecedented effort to maximize non-bureaucratic input into the foreign policy process in Canada, Mulroney created a special joint committee of both the House of Commons and the Senate. His secretary of state for external affairs, Joe Clark, led the effort by publishing a "green paper" on Canada's international relations that was intended to spark parliamentary and public discussion. Well over two hundred submissions were made to the special joint committee, which held hearings across the country. The result was a parliamentary report, to which the government issued a response. This process was so successful that the government used it subsequently to review Canada's development assistance policies.[11]

Ironically, the Mulroney government's defence review did not use this successful process, although it originally had planned to do so. However, that plan was derailed when DND kept delaying the writing of a draft of a green paper. Finally, in 1986, Perrin Beatty, the minister of national defence, decided in frustration to proceed directly to a white paper and have a new parliamentary committee on defence review the paper *ex post facto*.

The Liberals were sufficiently impressed with the Mulroney model that they adopted it in 1994–95 for their own defence and foreign policy reviews. However, the Chrétien government added an additional mechanism for the encouragement of public involvement: a national forum on Canada's international relations. The combination of the parliamentary committee and the national forum resulted in considerable public and parliamentary input into the defence white paper of 1994.

While the Martin and Harper reviews were produced by the defence establishment without the involvement of anyone outside government, the Trudeau government opened up the policy process somewhat in 2016. Harjit Sajjan appointed a four-person blue-ribbon panel to advise him: Bill Graham, a former minister of both defence and foreign affairs; Ray Henault, a former chief of defence staff; Louise Arbour, a former Supreme Court justice; and Margaret Purdy, a former deputy secretary for security and intelligence in the Privy Council Office. He also arranged for town hall and round-table meetings across the country, and he tasked parliamentary committees to assist in offering views on policy.

While the process that Harjit Sajjan initiated in 2016 was a positive step beyond the in-house practices of the Martin and Harper years, it can be argued that it did not go far enough. Rather, what is needed is a mechanism for an ongoing review of defence policy. The joint parliamentary committee model would provide an unparalleled opportunity to maximize bipartisanship, particularly given the reforms of the Senate introduced by the Trudeau government in 2015–16. A committee drawn from among the present Conservative caucus in the Senate, the "Senate Liberals"[12] and other independent senators, and the new, non-partisan senators appointed by Trudeau, together with MPs from all parties in the House of Commons, would provide a rich tapestry of perspectives on national defence.

Moreover, if such a committee were to be established as a *standing* joint committee rather than a one-off "special" committee, it would create an ongoing institution to provide ministers with the kind of feedback mechanism so necessary for a regular assessment of defence policy — and hence defence procurement. However, such a Standing Joint Committee on Defence Policy would not try to engage in the oversight of particular projects; that could indeed be left to a House of Commons committee of the sort recommended by Byers. Instead, this standing joint committee would take a much broader view of defence policy, seeking to articulate strategic goals for Canada.

Some may argue that the defence policy that would result from such a mechanism would be little more than the lowest common denominator among the various voices that would make themselves heard on defence issues. But there is no reason why a lowest-common-denominator policy would necessarily result from such a process. At last look, cabinets, whether Liberal or Conservative, have been quite capable of filtering the quank of contending policy perspectives, choosing among options, and making decisions. The proposal here does not suggest that ministers abdicate their responsibility to govern — in other words, to make choices. What it does suggest is that governments always have an opportunity to exercise judgment over which voices to listen to and which options to take seriously. And, for the Official Opposition, whether it be Liberal or Conservative, the incentive would be to help frame a defence policy that they would be comfortable to find in place were they to become the government.

At the same time, however, one of the purposes of listening to more than just the voice of the professional defence establishment, and listening in particular to the Official Opposition, is indeed to create a certain kind of common denominator in defence policy. Not the *lowest* common denominator, but a common denominator that large numbers of Canadians can support, and one that seeks to resolve the contradiction of defence policy in Canada by embracing a policy that reflects the security imaginary of Canadians, and one that seeks a special role for the Canadian Armed Forces.

The argument advanced in this chapter is a political scientist's argument. It does not deny the importance of paying attention to how institutions are structured or how their rules, incentives, and disincentives shape the behaviour of those who operate in them. Nor does it suggest that there are not reforms that could be applied to the way in which the defence procurement operates to make it better. What I do argue, however, is that a careful analysis of what causes the messes in Canadian defence procurement suggests that procedural tweaks will not be enough to resolve the problems. Grappling with the larger political environment in which procurement takes place offers, I suggest, a more promising starting point for better "mess management" in the future.

CONCLUSION:

GETTING IT RIGHT

Defence procurement is an inherently messy policy area. Experience in other countries suggests that Canada is by no means alone in experiencing difficulty securing for its military the right equipment, at the right price, and at the right time. But because of the big-eyes/empty-pockets contradiction identified in this book, it can be argued that the Canadian procurement mess is much more severe than it is in other countries and has more negative consequences for the military capabilities of the Canadian Armed Forces. Huge cost overruns, exceedingly long delays, needless expenditures — all mean that not only is the CAF not well-served, but Canadians generally are poorly served by the country's dysfunctional procurement system.

I have argued in this book that, to the extent that Canada's defence procurement mess can be fixed at all, it certainly cannot be fixed by just procedural or organizational tweaks. The analysis here suggests that the reasons for the mess might be multifarious, but many of the lines of analysis converge in what I have argued is the central problem in Canadian defence policy: the persistent unwillingness of governments, both Liberal and Conservative, to reconcile a series of contradictions. The main contradiction is that cabinets have been unwilling to admit that the model for the CAF that has been pressed on them by the defence establishment, and that they have, unthinkingly or not, accepted on the nod, is simply not achievable given the reality of the Canadian body politic. A fully integrated, multi-role, combat-capable CAF, equipped with state-of-the-art, modern systems, is, quite simply, beyond the reach of governments to pay for, given the persistent unwillingness of Canadians to tolerate defence expenditures during peacetime at anything other than paltry rates.

That central contradiction is compounded by others: the insistence of governments, both Liberal and Conservative, to see the principal purpose of defence procurement spending as the generation of economic benefits in Canada rather than the generation of military capability. Not only does this have a negative impact on capability, but it also makes equipment vastly more expensive than if the government just bought its military kit off the shelf. A third and related contradiction is the idea that weapons systems used by the CAF need to be "Canadianized"; however justifiable such modifications may be, Canadianization dramatically increases the costs of procurement.

From these three contradictions the defence procurement mess readily flows, and this mess is severely compounded by the propensity of Canadian politicians to politicize defence procurement, as Sam Hughes did in the early twentieth century, or as Jean Chrétien did at the end of the century, or as both the Conservatives and Liberals did with the CF-18 replacement more recently.

To manage the dysfunctions created by these contradictions, I have proposed that we need to focus on the political environment in which defence policy decisions — and thus defence procurement decisions — are made. More effective "mess management" leads inevitably to a focus on cabinet as the *principal* in the principal-agent relationship. The impact of the authority of cabinet, and in particular the prime minister, in shaping particular procurement decisions is clear: the impact of Pierre Elliott Trudeau and his cabinet on the New Fighter Aircraft program in the late 1970s and the impact of Stephen Harper on the evolution of the National Shipbuilding Procurement Strategy show us how political authority, clearly and unambiguously applied, can make a difference to both the policy process and to policy outcomes.

But in the area of defence policy, cabinet authority needs to be holistically applied, which leads to the mechanism of the defence white paper. I place considerable emphasis on this mechanism as the most promising approach to mess management in defence procurement because it seeks to tackle the root causes of the procurement mess. If the root cause is the political leadership, as I have argued, then a mechanism that can be readily used by the political leadership commends itself.

To be sure, Canada's political leaders have always used defence papers for domestic political purposes, as periodic ways to spin a new government's differences from its predecessor, and the most recent defence review by the government of Justin Trudeau is no different. But nothing should prevent Canadian political leaders in the two major parties from taking the opportunity of transforming the review overseen by Harjit Sajjan into a proper defence white paper and thereby recasting the role of such papers in Canadian politics.

I suggest that the most important function for a defence white paper is that it reflect the beliefs and perspectives of the ministers in cabinet. If ministers allow the defence establishment to set the parameters of Canada's defence policy, we will never resolve the core contradiction, since the Canadian Armed Forces and the Department of National Defence cannot, by themselves, make decisions about how to grow smaller and more specialized in order to fit within the budgetary limits imposed by a stingy citizenry. Because a military that is not fully multi-role is simply inconsistent with the professional self-perception of most serving officers, we should not be surprised that the military establishment is not well placed to engage in swingeing cuts in mission and function. Only cabinet can make those decisions.

In other countries, defence white papers are used as a way of helping guide procurement decisions, since procurement naturally flows from any white paper that is written for geostrategic rather than domestic political reasons. I argue that Canadians should adopt this best practice and begin to produce defence white papers at regular intervals. In this way, the verities about world politics and Canada's place in the world that are embraced at one particular point in time can be subjected to formalized regular review so that policies — and, if necessary, procurements — can be adjusted. (And if the world hasn't changed in the intervening period, and no adjustment is necessary, little will have been lost.)

If cabinets are going to embrace the defence white paper approach, then going beyond the defence establishment for setting the broad outlines of defence policy, I have argued, is a crucial step. For cabinets to be able to get both defence policy, and then defence procurement, "right," they need input from a wider variety of sources. Listening to, and taking advice from,

Canada's military professionals is critical, but it cannot be the only source, for reasons outlined in the previous chapter.

Perhaps the most important "outside" perspective, I have argued, is that of the Official Opposition. Integral to the mess-management strategy that has been proposed in this book is the idea of bipartisanship, since both the major parties, alternating in power, inevitably find themselves deeply intertwined by the long time horizons of defence procurement. Once again, it is sobering to reflect that the government that will close out the Sea King replacement will be whatever government is elected in the October 2019 elections — and it will be in the middle of its mandate in the 43rd Parliament. That will be nearly thirty years after the highly politicized cancellation of the EH101 helicopter contract in 1993 by the Liberal government of Jean Chrétien, and just over forty-five years since the replacement program began under the Liberal government of Pierre Elliott Trudeau. But a bipartisan approach to defence policy and the procurement that flows from defence policy decisions, I have suggested, is a rational approach for both the governing party and the Official Opposition, since defence procurement intertwines their futures.

If the Official Opposition is to be listened to by the government on defence matters, it is important to select the right mechanism for such bipartisanship. I have proposed the model introduced by the Progressive Conservative government of Brian Mulroney — a joint parliamentary committee that would receive a green paper on defence from the government, conduct public hearings, and present a report to the government for consideration in the government's own defence white paper process. This model was also embraced, in the 1990s, by the Chrétien Liberals, who used it to good effect as well.

In the 1980s and 1990s, involving the Senate in the policy-making process was a natural and smart move, because the upper house had by then earned a well-deserved reputation for its thoughtful contributions to policy discussions. Today, there are additional and equally compelling reasons for proposing to include senators in a new joint mechanism created to contribute to the development of defence policy. The newly appointed "non-partisan" senators, together with the Conservative caucus in the Senate and the "Senate Liberals," constitute a political resource that should not be overlooked if one wants to shape a defence policy that is not only as bipartisan as possible, but also as "pan-Canadian" as possible (in the sense that it is a policy that will resonate with as many Canadians as possible).

But unlike the joint committees in the 1980s and 1990s, which were one-off "special" committees, I propose that a new Standing Joint Committee on Defence Policy be created as a standing committee of parliament, so that it could remain in place to review defence policy, to develop an institutional memory, and to provide ongoing feedback to the government on changes that might, in the committee's view, be needed in light of changes in the geostrategic environment.

Finally, I argue that the final piece in the approach suggested here is the resolution of the core contradiction in Canadian defence policy: aligning the size and complexity of the CAF with the slim resources that Canadian citizens are willing to devote to defence. I have argued that the cheapness of Canadians is an unalterable given in defence policy, and that nothing short of a dramatic change in geostrategic circumstances will change that cheapness. That may strike some as defeatist, but there is nothing in Canadian history to suggest that Canadians would find an appeal to provide the CAF with the resources necessary to create and sustain a state-of-the-art multi-role force at all compelling.

I have suggested that the only way to resolve this contradiction is to embrace a defence policy that is written for easy-riding Canadians rather than for the Canadian military establishment. If Canadians are not going to provide the CAF with the funds necessary to sustain a proper multi-role military — and they are not — then it is time that we cut our military coat according to our cloth. This means a defence policy that could well continue to embrace the roles usually assigned to the armed forces by the government — defending Canada, defending North America, and contributing to international peace and security — but the procurement implications of each of these roles would be significantly different. Only in the case of North American defence are there true imperatives in procurement: the RCAF *must* fly fighters with capabilities that are acceptable to the United States, and the RCN *must* have vessels that are able to defend the maritime approaches to North America to American satisfaction. In all other roles, however, the government has the luxury of discretionary choices in what the CAF can and should contribute.

But a trade-off is also proposed here: whatever future roles might be selected for the Canadian Armed Forces, there would be a commitment that the "coat" would be maintained at a world-class standard, always provided with state-of-the-art equipment. This would ensure that even if Canada remains a spending laggard in multilateral organizations like NATO, never coming even close to the 2 percent of GDP target set by the alliance, it would be still able to contribute meaningful and effective hard power to coalition operations.

❖

I recognize that the argument advanced in this book — that a change of political culture among elected representatives in the Liberal and Conservative parties will be necessary before the messes in Canadian defence procurement can be cleaned up — involves a considerable leap of faith. For Canadian politicians have come by their attitudes and their behaviour on defence procurement through the weight of historical experience, something that clearly demonstrates to them certain immutable verities about what works and what doesn't work in Canadian politics.

But the dysfunctions in defence procurement in Canada — the massive waste of resources because of delays, or because decisions are made for reasons other than national defence, or because politicians play politics with defence procurement decisions — and the constant degradation in the capabilities of the Canadian Armed Forces that these dysfunctions have created, convince me that there must be a better way to organize ourselves.

While it is clear that there can never be a complete "fix" for any country's defence procurement system, the *political* suggestions laid out here, based on an analysis of the Canadian experience, provide, I believe, a viable road map for the political leadership in Canada to follow to recast defence policy — and in the process eliminate much of the mess that has so marked the defence procurement system.

Political leaders in Canada always talk a good line about how they "manage taxpayer dollars responsibly" and always provide the "best equipment" to "our brave men and women in uniform." A look at the record suggests that our governors have all too often failed both taxpayers and the members of the Canadian Armed Forces. It is time that our political leaders move to transform their feel-good talking points into reality and begin to get defence procurement right.

POSTSCRIPT

This essay on the problems in Canada's contemporary defence procurement was completed in the summer of 2016, but it has its origins in one of the key defence procurements of the late 1970s: the acquisition of the new fighter aircraft discussed in Chapter 2. During the middle decades of the Cold War, the Canadian air force maintained two different fleets of fighters: CF-101 Voodoo interceptors defended North America against the possibility of attack by Soviet bombers, and CF-104 Starfighter ground attack/nuclear strike aircraft were stationed in Europe as part of Canada's contribution to the North Atlantic Treaty Organization to deter a possible Soviet attack on western Europe. By the end of the 1970s, both fleets, which had entered service in the early 1960s, were coming to the end of their lives, and so the Liberal government of Pierre Elliott Trudeau decided that it was time to replace both fleets simultaneously. However, the Trudeau government decided that a single fighter that could perform both interception and ground attack roles would be acquired. It launched the New Fighter Aircraft (NFA) program in 1977, and three years later, in April 1980, cabinet selected the F/A-18 Hornet, a fighter built by the McDonnell Douglas Corporation. Between 1982 and 1988, 138 Hornets, officially designated by the Canadian Armed Forces as the CF-188, were delivered to Canada.

At the time, I was a young and callow professor in the Department of Political Science at McMaster University in Hamilton, teaching Canadian foreign and defence policy. Even before the final decision was made, one of my colleagues at McMaster, Michael M. Atkinson, a public policy expert, and I decided to research the decision-making process that the Trudeau government had established for this acquisition. We were not so much interested in defence procurement as in the impact that the political authority vested in cabinet ministers could have on bureaucrats and bureaucratic decisions. For we were very aware that the Trudeau government had been badly burned by bureaucrats in the Department of National Defence on an earlier defence procurement, the long-range patrol aircraft (LRPA). Our research, subsequently published in *Canadian Public Administration,*** revealed that the Trudeau cabinet had learned important lessons from the LRPA: the way that it managed the NFA project made that procurement a model defence procurement, one that was consistently praised.

In the years that followed, neither Atkinson nor I continued our work on defence procurement. He went on to become one of Canada's foremost specialists in public policy; my specialty was

---

* Atkinson and Nossal, "Bureaucratic Politics and the New Fighter Aircraft Decisions," 531–62 (see chap. 2, n. 26).

Canadian foreign policy. But it was because of that early work on the NFA, carried out at the beginning of my academic career, that I watched with special interest as the CF-18s that we had studied in the late 1970s were coming to the end of their useful service lives. I could not help wondering whether the government in Ottawa, when it came time to replace the CF-18s, would look back to the last time a government had to replace a fighter aircraft and take on board those lessons that the Trudeau government had learned that had made the NFA procurement such a success.

And it was because of that earlier research that I watched — with the kind of morbid fascination that draws us to look at a bad accident — as the process of replacing the CF-18 became the trainwreck that it did under the Conservative government of Stephen Harper. It was clear that the Harper government did not bother looking back to the late 1970s to see how an earlier government had dealt with a major defence procurement; the Conservatives obviously did not think that the Liberals had anything to teach them about governing.

This hubris has had significant negative consequences. The Conservative government's unwillingness to learn from the past resulted in the CF-18 replacement program drifting off the rails — with a lot of help, to be sure, from the Liberal opposition, which delighted in politicizing and delegitimizing the Conservative procurement. But it was only after the derailment that the Harper government introduced the kind of governance structure that the Trudeau government had employed in the late 1970s.

Wanting to make sense of the failed procurement, I found myself writing another article on another "new fighter aircraft," this one at the other end of my academic career.[*]

---

[*] Nossal, "Late Learners," 167–84 (see chap. 2, n. 11).

Looking at the F-35 procurement, I concluded that the Harper government's efforts to shift gears had come too late: the F-35 procurement was irreparably compromised. And it has remained compromised, since Justin Trudeau, the Liberal prime minister who took power in November 2015, has decided to continue to play politics with the CF-18 replacement.

It was the process of looking at the F-35 fiasco that prompted me to take a closer look at the pattern of Canadian defence procurement between the successful NFA acquisition in the late 1970s and the F-35 procurement. And looking at Canadian defence procurement more generally revealed clearly that the CF-18 replacement fiasco was part of a larger pattern of dysfunction that was endemic under both Liberal and Conservative governments. While every country struggles to get defence procurement right, Canada seems to get it less right than others. This book is an attempt to explain why the successors of Trudeau *père* could not consistently replicate the success of the NFA decision, and why the incredible waste of resources has become so normal that governments can and do throw hundreds of millions of dollars away, seemingly without a second thought, and certainly without ever suffering any political consequences.

But it was not just scholarly curiosity that prompted this book. As a citizen, I was angered by the negative effects of the political gamesmanship that pervades defence procurement in this country: the waste of scarce resources that could be used more productively; the diminution of Canada's military capabilities, which in turn diminishes our capacity in global affairs; and, most importantly, the risks to the soldiers, sailors, and aviators who are put in harm's way by Canada's governors with equipment that too often is aging, rusted out, or simply inappropriate for the task at hand. And thus this book was written in the hope that other Canadians would begin to question why governments in Ottawa continue to insist on playing politics with defence procurement, and why they can't do better when it comes to equipping the Canadian Armed Forces.

All authors are invariably indebted, and deeply so, to those who help turn an idea into a book, and I am no different. I wanted to begin by thanking those who were at the forefront of that transformation — the committed team at Dundurn Press. Patrick Boyer, the general editor of the Point of View series, was unstinting in his encouragement and support of an exploration of this important topic. Readers of this book should not be surprised: Patrick is a Canadian who has spent much of the last four decades deeply engaged in public policy — as a member of parliament, an academic, a broadcaster, a publisher, and an activist. I am most grateful to Dominic Farrell, my editor at Dundurn, for all that he did to make me appear more logical than I really am; his advice improved this book in numerous ways that will remain completely invisible to the reader. The copy editor, Jenny Govier, had an eagle eye for errors and infelicities, and a deft touch. The production editor, Cheryl Hawley, kept the book on track despite the changes in Canadian defence policy that kept unfolding over the summer of 2016. I would like to thank Carrie Gleason, the editorial director, not only for helping shape the book from the outset, but also for her skills with difficult-to-work-with polymer. And to Margaret Bryant and Kendra Martin, my thanks in advance for what can only come long after these words are written.

During the writing of the book, I was fortunate to have the help of a number of colleagues who were willing to share their expertise with me. Ron Haycock, of the Royal Military College of Canada, was a wonderful source of knowledge on the politics of the Ross rifle. I also want to thank Tony Griffiths of Sydney, Australia, for his help on something that, because of his expertise, doesn't even appear in the book: the "Enfield inch." This refers to the definition of an inch used by the Royal Small Arms Factory at Enfield Lock in the United Kingston between 1860 and 1923 that differed from an Imperial standard inch by four-tenths of a thousandth of an inch (0.00040"). Lee-Enfields were manufactured using the Enfield inch and Ross rifles were manufactured using the Imperial standard inch, and in the search for the reasons for the tendency of the Ross rifles to jam, it has been hypothesized that the difference might have been a factor. While the Enfield inch did indeed create some problems for those who sought to manufacture Lee-Enfield rifles elsewhere,[*] Tony was able to clarify that the Enfield inch could not have been

---

[*] The difference proved to be a problem when the Australian government decided to manufacture Lee-Enfield rifles using machine tools purchased from Pratt & Whitney in the United States rather than from the Royal Small Arms Factory. Considerable delays were encountered when American and Australian engineers could not reconcile the differences between the measurements on the sealed drawings that they received from Enfield Lock and the actual dimensions of the test rifles that accompanied them. For the story, see Tony Griffiths, *The Enfield Inch and the Lithgow .303* (Terrey Hills, NSW: Toptech Engineering, 2003).

responsible for the Ross rifle's tendency to jam. First, while the Lee-Enfield rifle itself was manufactured using the Enfield inch, the .303-inch ammunition it used was manufactured using the Imperial standard inch. Moreover, even if the .303-inch ammunition used by the Ross had been manufactured using the Enfield inch, the minuscule four-tenths of a thousandth of an inch difference would not have made any difference to the firing of the weapon. In short, Tony suggested that the blame for the jamming discussed in Chapter 1 must lie elsewhere.

My thanks to my good friend and colleague, Donald Story of the University of Saskatchewan, who is Canada's foremost scholarly expert on the CF-105 Arrow. Nearly sixty years on, the Avro Arrow remains an iconically contentious issue in Canada. It is also the subject of a number of conspiracy theories, including the persistent belief that although all prototypes of the Arrow were ordered destroyed after the cancellation of the program, a prototype of the Arrow was secretly spirited away and remains hidden somewhere. My thanks to Don for helping me navigate those shoals. And my appreciation to Andrew Davies of the Australian Strategic Policy Institute in Canberra, for sharing with me his expertise on the F-35.

Finally, I would like to thank those members of the public service and the Canadian Armed Forces — both serving and former — who have helped shape my views on defence procurement. I must start by doing something that thirty-seven years ago Mike Atkinson and I could not do: publicly thank Gen. Paul Manson. One of the many positions that General Manson held before he became chief of the defence staff in 1986 was the manager of the New Fighter Aircraft program, and he selflessly and candidly gave two young academics a great deal of (off-the-record) time and help. We were of course not permitted to acknowledge it then, but I can thank him now.

More recently, I benefitted tremendously from the insights, suggestions, and criticisms offered by participants at seminars at the Centre for Foreign Policy Studies at Dalhousie University and the Centre for International and Defence Policy and the School of Policy Studies at Queen's University. My deepest thanks to all of you.

KRN

Howe Island, Ontario

ABBREVIATIONS AND ACRONYMS

ADM	assistant deputy minister
AIT	Agreement on Internal Trade
AOPS	Arctic/offshore patrol ship
AOR	auxiliary oil replenishment
ASW	anti-submarine warfare
BQ	Bloc Québécois
CA	Canadian Alliance
CADSI	Canadian Association of Defence and Security Industries
CAF	Canadian Armed Forces
CCV	close combat vehicle
CDAI	Conference of Defence Associations Institute
CF	Canadian Forces
CFB	Canadian Forces base
COTS	commercial off-the-shelf
CPC	Conservative Party of Canada
CSC	Canadian surface combatant

DART	Disaster Assistance Response Team
DND	Department of National Defence
DPS	Defence Procurement Strategy
GDP	gross domestic product
GST	Goods and Services Tax
HiG	Hizb-i-Islami Gulbuddin
HMCS	Her Majesty's Canadian Ship (or Submarine)
HMMWV	high mobility multi-purpose wheeled vehicle (aka Humvee)
IED	improvised explosive device
IRB	industrial and regional benefits
ISIL	Islamic State in Iraq and the Levant
IT&C	Department of Industry, Trade and Commerce
ITB	industrial and technological benefits
JSF	joint strike fighter
JSS	joint support ship
JUSTAS	joint unmanned surveillance target acquisition system
KICs	key industrial capabilities
LAV	light armoured vehicle
LRPA	long-range patrol aircraft
LUVW	light utility vehicle wheeled
MilCOTS	militarized commercial off-the-shelf
NATO	North Atlantic Treaty Organization
NDHQ	National Defence Headquarters
NDP	New Democratic Party
NFA	new fighter aircraft
NHL	National Hockey League
NORAD	North American Aerospace Defense Command

NSA	new shipborne aircraft
NSH	new search-and-rescue helicopter
NSPS	National Shipbuilding Procurement Strategy
NWS	North Warning System
PBO	parliamentary budget officer
PC	Progressive Conservative
PMO	Prime Minister's Office
PRT	Provincial Reconstruction Team
PSPC	Public Services and Procurement Canada
PWGSC	Public Works and Government Services Canada
RCAF	Royal Canadian Air Force
RCN	Royal Canadian Navy
RFP	request for proposals
RN	Royal Navy (United Kingdom)
RNZAF	Royal New Zealand Air Force
SAR	search and rescue
SMP	standard military pattern
SOR	statement of requirements
TAPV	tactical armoured patrol vehicle
UAV	unmanned aerial vehicle
UHF	ultra high frequency
U.K.	United Kingdom
USAF	U.S. Air Force
USN	U.S. Navy
VBSIED	vehicle-borne suicide IED

NOTES

FOREWORD

1. Ferry de Kerckhove, *The Strategic Outlook for Canada 2016*,
   Vimy Paper 27, CDAI, 2016; de Kerckhove, *The Strategic
   Outlook for Canada 2015*, Vimy Paper 22, CDAI, 2015; Ferry
   de Kerckhove and George Petrolekas, *The Strategic Outlook for
   Canada 2014*, Vimy Paper 7, CDAI, 2014; Petrolekas and de
   Kerckhove, *The Strategic Outlook for Canada*, Vimy Paper 6,
   CDAI, 2013.
2. One can sadistically dive into every piece written by David
   Perry on this subject to be convinced.
3. A very solid analysis of the whole F-35 saga by Richard
   Shimooka was published by the CDA Institute as this book
   went to press: *The Fourth Dimension: The F-35 Program, Defence
   Procurement, and the Conservative Government, 2006–2015*,
   Vimy Paper 33, September 2016, www.cdainstitute.ca/images/
   Vimy_Papers/Vimy_Paper_33.pdf.

INTRODUCTION

1. Dave Perry, "Putting the 'Armed' Back into the Canadian Armed Forces: Improving Defence Procurement in Canada," *Vimy Paper* 21 (January 2015).

2. Meagan Fitzpatrick, "Kevin Page Says Defence Purchasing 'Broken' and 'Wrong,'" *CBC News*, May 3, 2012, www.cbc.ca/news/politics/kevin-page-says-defence-purchasing-broken-and-wrong-1.1185882.

3. Dan Ross, "Is Defence Procurement Broken or Is This Normal?" *FrontLine Defence* 10, no. 6 (2013): 8–9, http://defence.frontline. online/article/2013/6/871-Is-Defence-Procurement-Broken-or-is-this-Normal; also quoted in Jeffrey Simpson, "How Broken Is Military Procurement? It's Time for a Blue-Ribbon Panel," *Globe and Mail*, March 16, 2013, and Lee Berthiaume, "Former Top Defence Official Dan Ross Defends His Handling of F-35 Jet Controversy," *Ottawa Citizen*, January 21, 2013.

4. Canada, Parliament, House of Commons, Standing Committee on National Defence, *Minutes of Proceedings*, 42nd Parl., 1st sess., Meeting no. 3, March 8, 2016, at 09:13:24.

5. Christyn Cianfarani, "Three Steps Toward Better Defence Procurement," *Policy Options*, January 12, 2016, http://policyoptions.irpp.org/issues/january-2016/three-steps-toward-better-defence-procurement.

6. Terry Milewski, "Davie Shipyard Boss Calls Canada's National Shipbuilding Strategy 'Bizarre,'" *CBC News*, March 17, 2016, www.cbc.ca/news/politics/davie-shipyard-boss-canada-shipbuilding-plan-bizarre-1.3494460.

7. David Perry, "Four Steps for Fixing Canada's Trouble-Prone Procurement System," *iPolitics*, February 8, 2016, https://ipolitics.ca/2016/02/08/dnp-four-steps-for-fixing-canadas-trouble-prone-procurement-system; Michael Byers, "Canada's Military Procurement like a Monty Python Movie," *Toronto Star*, October 9, 2013; Elinor Sloan, "Canadian Defence

Commitments: Overview and Status of Selected Acquisitions and Initiatives," *SPP Research Papers* 6, no. 36 (December 2013), www.policyschool.ca/wp-content/uploads/2016/03/e-sloan-canada-defence-revised.pdf; J. Craig Stone, "Improving the Acquisition Process in Canada," *SPP Research Papers* 8, no. 16 (April 2015), www.policyschool.ca/wp-content/uploads/2016/03/improving-acquisition-process-stone.pdf; Aude-Emmanuelle Fleurant and Yannick Quéau, "L'approvisionnement en armament du Canada: une vision parcellaire et des objectifs imprécis," *Options politiques*, January 21, 2016, http://policyoptions.irpp.org/issues/january-2016/lapprovisionnement-en-armement-du-canada-unevision-parcellaire-et-des-objectifs-imprecis.

8. Jeffrey Simpson, "A Long Line of Procurement Failures," *Globe and Mail*, January 22, 2014; Andrew Coyne, "Canada's Glorious Bipartisan Tradition of Messing Up Military Procurement," *National Post*, November 17, 2014; Alec Castonguay, "F-35: un rapport accablant," *l'Actualité*, April 3, 2012; Scott Gilmore, "Military Procurement Is a National Disgrace," *Maclean's*, June 19, 2015, www.macleans.ca/news/canada/military-procurement-is-a-national-disgrace.

9. The *Oxford English Dictionary* defines clusterfuck as coarse military slang for "a bungled or botched undertaking." First used during the Vietnam War in the 1960s, it was the etymological offspring of the equally coarse expression coined during the Second World War for chaotic, confused, or botched operations: snafu (situation normal: all fucked up). Jon Stewart, who hosted *The Daily Show*, a nightly news parody, from 1999 to 2015, helped popularize the word beyond the military by using it frequently in his routines (though it invariably appeared onscreen as "clusterf#@k").

10. Aaron Plamondon, *The Politics of Procurement: Military Acquisition in Canada and the* Sea King *Helicopter* (Vancouver: UBC Press, 2010), x.

11. A Major Crown Project is a very large procurement that has an estimated cost exceeding $100 million and has been deemed

"high risk" by the Treasury Board. For the current status of DND/CAF Major Crown Projects, see www.forces.gc.ca/en/about-reports-pubs-report-plan-priorities/2015-status-report-transformational-major-crown-projects.page#P22.

12. Russell L. Ackoff, *Redesigning the Future: A Systems Approach to Societal Problems* (New York: John Wiley & Sons, 1974), chaps. 1–2; "The Future of Operational Research Is Past," *Journal of the Operational Research Society* 30, no. 2 (February 1979): 99–100.

13. The idea that there are some policy problems that are so complex they cannot be resolved was originally proposed by Horst W.J. Rittel and Melvin M. Webber, "Dilemmas in a General Theory of Planning," *Policy Sciences* 4, no. 2 (1973): 155–69. For a good contemporary discussion, see Brian W. Head, "Wicked Problems in Public Policy," *Public Policy* 3, no. 2 (2008): 101–18.

14. Alan S. Williams, *Reinventing Canadian Defence Procurement: A View from the Inside* (Montreal and Kingston: Breakout Educational Network/School of Policy Studies, Queen's University/McGill-Queen's University Press, 2006), chaps. 1–4; also Craig Stone, "Defence Procurement and Industry," in *Canada's National Security in the Post–9/11 World: Strategy, Interests, and Threats*, ed. David S. McDonough (Toronto: University of Toronto Press, 2012), 73–97.

1: GETTING IT WRONG: A CENTURY OF DEFENCE PROCUREMENT MESSES

1. Williams, *Reinventing Canadian Defence Procurement*, iv and 87.

2. Details on the Ross are from A.M. Willms, "Decision Making: The Case of the Ross Rifle," *Canadian Public Administration* 2, no. 4 (December 1959), 202–13; Ronald G. Haycock and B.D. Hunt, "Early Canadian Weapons Acquisition: 'That Damned Ross Rifle,'" *Canadian Defence Quarterly* 14, no. 3 (Winter 1984–85), 48–57; Carman Miller, *A Knight in Politics: A Biography of Sir Frederick Borden* (Montreal and Kingston:

    McGill-Queen's University Press, 2010), 216–24; and R. Blake Brown, *Arming and Disarming: A History of Gun Control in Canada* (Toronto: University of Toronto Press, 2012), 116–17.

3. Haycock and Hunt, "'That Damned Ross Rifle,'" 49.

4. Carman Miller, *Painting the Map Red: Canada and the South African War, 1899–1902* (Montreal and Kingston: McGill-Queen's University Press, 1993), 439.

5. Ronald G. Haycock, *Sam Hughes: The Public Career of a Controversial Canadian, 1885–1916* (Waterloo: Wilfrid Laurier Press, 1986), 123.

6. For a demonstration of how easy it was to reassemble a Ross bolt incorrectly, see www.youtube.com/watch?v=EaSui_UqDX8.

7. Sharon Adams, "The Ross Rifle," *Legion Magazine*, February 16, 2016.

8. Haycock, *Sam Hughes*, 250.

9. The exchange was immediately published on Borden's orders in pamphlet form by the Liberal party; see http://wartimecanada.ca/sites/default/files/documents/Hughes%20%26%20Borden.pdf.

10. Haycock and Hunt, "'That Damned Ross Rifle.'"

11. The most authoritative accounts, based on cabinet documents, are: Donald C. Story and Russell Isinger, "The Origins of the Cancellation of Canada's Avro CF-105 Arrow Fighter Program: A Failure of Strategy," *Journal of Strategic Studies* 30, no. 6 (2007), 1025–50; and Russell Isinger, "The Avro Canada VF-105 Arrow Programme: Decisions and Determinants" (MA thesis, University of Saskatchewan, 1997). Also see Jon B. McLin, *Canada's Changing Defense Policy, 1957–1963: The Problems of a Middle Power in Alliance* (Toronto: Copp Clark, 1967), 61–84.

12. For an exploration of this phenomenon, see Jean-Christophe Boucher and Kim Richard Nossal, *Home Game: The Domestic Politics of Canada's Afghanistan Mission* (Vancouver: submitted to UBC Press, 2016).

13. Carlotta Gall, *The Wrong Enemy: America in Afghanistan, 2001–2014* (Boston: Houghton Mifflin Harcourt, 2015).

14. Paul Koring, "U.S. Warned Canadians Not to Use Flimsy Jeeps," *Globe and Mail*, October 4, 2003.

15. Sean M. Maloney, *The Canadian Army in Afghanistan*, vol. 1: *A Nation under Fire, 2001–2006* (Kingston: Canadian Defence Academy Press, 2016), chap. 4.

16. Stephen Thorne, "Canadian Troops Leave for Afghanistan," *Canadian Press*, July 19, 2003; see also Canada, Parliament, House of Commons, *Debates*, 37th Parl., 2nd sess., October 6, 2003, 14h25.

17. House of Commons, *Debates*, 37th Parl., 2nd sess., October 3, 2003, 11h20, and October 6, 2003, 14h15, 14h25, and 14h40.

18. House of Commons, *Debates*, 37th Parl., 2nd sess., October 30, 2003, 19h20.

19. House of Commons, *Debates*, 37th Parl., 3rd sess., May 4, 2004, 10h05.

20. Colin Freeze, "Iltis Jeep Blameless in Soldiers' Deaths, Review Finds," *Globe and Mail*, August 25, 2004.

21. Sean Maloney, *Fighting for Afghanistan: A Rogue Historian at War* (Annapolis: Naval Institute Press, 2011), 27.

22. This section is based on: David Pugliese, "Politics, Bureaucracy, and Two Dead Soldiers: Why Our Troops Don't Have the Wheels They Need," *Ottawa Citizen*, October 11, 2003; Williams, *Reinventing Canadian Defence Procurement*, 9–10; and Sharon Hobson, "Canada Awaits Sole Response to Vehicle Request," *Jane's Defence Weekly*, May 9, 2001.

23. Sean M. Maloney and John Llambias, *Chances for Peace: Canadian Soldiers in the Balkans, 1992–1995: An Oral History* (St. Catharines, ON: Vanwell, 2002); Nicholas Gammer, *From Peacekeeping to Peacemaking: Canada's Response to the Yugoslav Crisis* (Montreal and Kingston: McGill-Queen's University Press, 2001).

24. House of Commons, *Debates*, 35th Parl., 1st sess., January 25, 1994, 17h00.

25. Marc Milner, *Canada's Navy: The First Century* (Toronto: University of Toronto Press, 1999).

26. "Used Subs a 'Daft' Deal for Canada, U.K. MP Says," *CBC News*, March 15, 2012, www.cbc.ca/news/canada/nova-scotia/used-subs-a-daft-deal-for-canada-u-k-mp-says-1.1166047; "Used U.K. Submarines Prompted Compensation Demand," *CBC News*, May 2, 2012, www.cbc.ca/news/canada/nova-scotia/used-u-k-submarines-prompted-compensation-demand-1.1270576.

27. For example, Michael Byers and Stewart Webb, *That Sinking Feeling: Canada's Submarine Program Springs a Leak* (Ottawa: Canadian Centre for Policy Alternatives, 2013); for reactions, see Paul T. Mitchell, "Full of Holes: Byers and Webb on the Canada's Submarine Programme," *Policy Update*, Canadian Defence and Foreign Affairs Institute, July 2013; Nathan M. Greenfield, "Under Pressure: In Defence of Canada's Submarines," *The Walrus*, March 23, 2015.

2: GETTING IT ALL WRONG: THE SEA KING AND F-35 FIASCOS

1. The best examination of this procurement down to 2010 is Aaron Plamondon, *The Politics of Procurement: Military Acquisition in Canada and the* Sea King *Helicopter* (Vancouver: UBC Press, 2010).

2. Ross Howard and Kevin Cox, "Québec to Receive Lion's Share of $4.4 Billion Helicopter Deal: Controversial Project Sparks Wave of Protest," *Globe and Mail*, July 25, 1992.

3. Jeff Sallot and Ross Howard, "PM Chops Seven Helicopters," *Globe and Mail*, September 3, 1993; and Kirk Makin, "Chrétien Questions Campbell Ability after PC Shifting," *Globe and Mail*, September 14, 1993. Also see Plamondon, *Politics of Procurement*, 125.

4. EH Industries was paid $136.6 million for work in progress and $21.2 million in cancellation penalties; Loral Electronics, which had acquired Paramax in 1995, was paid $98.4 million for work in progress and $67.5 million in cancellation

penalties. Both companies had already received a total $154.6 million for the project definition phase. Plamondon, *Politics of Procurement*, 150.

5. Jean Chrétien, *My Years as Prime Minister* (Toronto: Vintage Canada, 2007), 54.

6. Hugh Winsor, "Copter Deal Splits Losers, Winners," *Globe and Mail*, January 7, 1998.

7. Plamondon, *Politics of Procurement*, 154.

8. Williams, *Reinventing Canadian Defence Procurement*, 43.

9. "MacKay Says Chopper Deal 'Worst' in Canada's History," *CBC News*, July 10, 2012, www.cbc.ca/news/canada/mackay-says-chopper-deal-worst-in-canada-s-history-1.1132899.

10. David Pugliese, "DND Concerned about New Cyclone Helicopter's Engines," *Ottawa Citizen*, June 19, 2015.

11. Kim Richard Nossal, "Late Learners: The F-35 and Lessons from the New Fighter Aircraft Program," *International Journal* 68, no. 1 (Winter 2012–13), 167–84.

12. David Pugliese, "Tories Change Strategy for Pitching Stealth Fighter," *Ottawa Citizen*, April 4, 2011.

13. Liberal Party of Canada, "Liberals Will Cancel F-35 Deal and Hold an Open Competition," October 27, 2010.

14. Daniel Leblanc, "Harper Bending to U.S. on Sole-Source Fighter Purchase, Documents Reveal," *Globe and Mail*, June 11, 2010.

15. Canada, Parliament, Parliamentary Budget Officer, *An Estimate of the Fiscal Impact of Canada's Proposed Acquisition of the F-35 Lightning II Joint Strike Fighter*, March 10, 2011.

16. Canada, Office of the Auditor General of Canada, "Replacing Canada's Fighter Jets," chap. 2 in *Report of the Auditor General of Canada to the House of Commons*, Spring 2012, www.oag-bvg.gc.ca/internet/docs/parl_oag_201204_02_e.pdf.

17. Canada, National Defence and the Canadian Armed Forces, "Government of Canada Announces Comprehensive Response to Chapter 2 of the 2012 Spring Report of the Auditor General of Canada," Statement NR 12.043, April 3, 2012, www.forces.gc.ca/en/news/article.page?doc=government-of-canada-

announces-comprehensive-response-to-chapter-2-of-the-2012-spring-report-of-the-auditor-general-of-canada/hir3oy82.

18. Jeffrey Simpson, "F-35 Fiasco Knocks Conservative Spin off Its Axis," *Globe and Mail*, December 8, 2012.

19. John Ivison, "'We're Looking at All the Options,'" *National Post*, November 24, 2012.

20. "Fighter Jet Plan 'Reset' as F-35 Costs Soar," *CBC News*, December 12, 2012, www.cbc.ca/news/politics/fighter-jet-plan-reset-as-f-35-costs-soar-1.1203373.

21. Speaking in French, Trudeau claimed that the Harper Conservatives "se sont accrochés à un avoin qui ne fonctionne pas et qui est loin de pouvoir foctionner," which Hansard translated as "The Conservatives threw their lot in with a plane that does not work and is a long way from ever working." House of Commons, Debates, 42nd Parl., 1st Sess., June 7, 2016, 14h20; Lee Berthiaume, "Liberals Planning to Buy Super Hornet Fighter Jets Before Making Final Decision on F-35s, Sources Say," *National Post*, June 6, 2016.

22. Lee Berthiaume, "Harjit Sajjan Going Back to Drawing Board on Fighter Jets, Launching Consultations," *CBC News*, July 6, 2016.

23. Lee Berthiaume, "Liberals Make $33M Payment to Stay in F-35 Program," *Toronto Star*, 26 July 2016.

24. Matthew Fisher, "Why the Super Hornets Will Force Canada out of Its Own North," *National Post*, June 12, 2016.

25. In particular, the industrial offset package: see James Fergusson, "In Search of a Strategy: The Evolution of Canadian Defence Industrial and Regional Benefits Policy," in *The Economics of Offsets: Defence Procurement and Countertrade*, ed. Stephen Martin (London: Routledge, 1996), 114–15. Industrial offsets are discussed in the next chapter.

26. Michael M. Atkinson and Kim Richard Nossal, "Bureaucratic Politics and the New Fighter Aircraft Decisions," *Canadian Public Administration* 24 (Winter 1981): 531–62; Martin Shadwick, "Comparison Shopping," *Canadian Military Journal* 10, no. 4 (Autumn 2010), 80–82; and Anton Bezglasnyy and

Douglas Alan Ross, "Strategically Superfluous, Unacceptably Overpriced: The Case Against Canada's F-35A Lightning II Acquisition," *Canadian Foreign Policy Journal* 17, no. 3 (September 2011), 241.

27. Canada, Parliament, House of Commons, Standing Committee on National Defence, *Procurement and Associated Processes*, 39th Parl., 2nd sess., February 2008, 3.

28. David Pugliese, "Army Trucks Project Cancelled after DND Added $300 million to Price Tag Without Permission," *Postmedia News*, July 17, 2012.

3: EXPLAINING THE MESS

1. Williams, *Reinventing Canadian Defence Procurement*, 72.

2. David Perry, "Fixing Procurement," *2016 Policy Review Series*, Canadian Global Affairs Institute, July 2016, 1.

3. Perry, "Four Steps for Fixing Canada's Trouble-Prone Procurement System" (see Introduction, n. 7).

4. For a discussion, see Michael Tucker, *Canadian Foreign Policy: Contemporary Issues and Themes* (Toronto: McGraw-Hill Ryerson, 1980), 155–63.

5. In April 1978, the Ontario Supreme Court rejected Goyer's arguments that his accusations, both inside and outside the House of Commons, were covered by parliamentary privilege, and it awarded Stopforth $10,000. However, that decision was subsequently overturned on appeal in April 1979, the Ontario Court of Appeal ruling that the minister's remarks to reporters outside the Commons were in fact an extension of his parliamentary privilege.

6. Stephen Martin, "Countertrade and Offsets: An Overview of the Theory and Evidence," in *The Economics of Offsets: Defence Procurement and Countertrade*, ed. Stephen Martin (London: Routledge, 1996), 31–32.

7. James Fergusson, "In Search of a Strategy: The Evolution of

Canadian Defence Industrial and Regional Benefits Policy," in Martin, ed., *Economics of Offsets*, 107–38.

8. The NSPS, announced on June 3, 2010, sought to have both large and small ships built for the RCN and the Canadian Coast Guard built in Canada. See www.tpsgc-pwgsc.gc.ca/app-acq/amd-dp/mer-sea/sncn-nss/index-eng.html. The NSPS is discussed in the next chapter.

9. Review of Federal Support to Research and Development, *Innovation Canada: A Call to Action — Expert Panel Report* (Ottawa: n.d. [2011]). The report was named after the chair of the panel, Tom Jenkins, CEO of Open Text in Waterloo. The panel produced a special report on procurement: http://rd-review.ca/eic/site/033.nsf/eng/h_00317.html.

10. Pierre Lagueux, "The Defence Procurement Market is Unlike Any Other," *Policy Options*, January 12, 2016, http://policyoptions.irpp.org/issues/january-2016/the-defence-procurement-market-is-unlike-any-other.

11. David Rudd, "Off-the-Shelf or New Design? Considerations for the Canadian Surface Combatant Program," *Canadian Military Journal* 16, no. 1 (Winter 2015), 5–13.

12. Jutta Weldes, *Constructing National Interests: The United States and the Cuban Missile Crisis* (Minneapolis: University of Minnesota Press, 1999), 10; Kim Richard Nossal, "Rethinking the Security Imaginary: Canadian Security and the Case of Afghanistan," in *Locating Global Order: American Power and Canadian Security after 9/11*, ed. Bruno Charbonneau and Wayne S. Cox (Vancouver: UBC Press, 2010), 107–25.

13. House of Commons, *Debates*, February 21, 1875, 153; quoted in Desmond Morton, "Defending the Indefensible: Some Historical Perspectives on Canadian Defence, 1867–1987," *International Journal* 42, no. 4 (Autumn 1987), 643.

14. Morton, "Defending the Indefensible," 628.

15. Joel S. Sokolsky, "Realism Canadian Style: National Security Policy and the Chrétien Legacy," *Policy Matters* 5, no. 2

(June 2004): 11, http://irpp.org/wp-content/uploads/assets/ pmvol5no2.pdf.

16. NATO, "Defence Expenditures of NATO Countries (2008– 2015)," press release, January 28, 2016: 2, www.nato.int/nato_ static_fl2014/assets/pdf/pdf_2016_01/20160129_160128-pr- 2016-11-eng.pdf.

17. Milewski, "Davie Shipyard Boss Calls Canada's National Shipbuilding Strategy 'Bizarre'" (see Introduction, n. 6).

18. Norrin M. Ripsman, "Big Eyes and Empty Pockets: The Two Phrases of Conservative Defence Policy," in *Diplomatic Departures: The Conservative Era in Canadian Foreign Policy, 1984–93*, ed. Nelson Michaud and Kim Richard Nossal (Vancouver: UBC Press, 2001), 100–12.

4: REFORMING THE SYSTEM?

1. J. Ronald Fox, *Defense Acquisition Reform, 1960–2009: An Elusive Goal* (Washington, DC: Center of Military History, United States Army, 2011), xii.

2. Williams, *Reinventing Canadian Defence Procurement*.

3. Ibid., 67–68.

4. Michael Byers, *Smart Defence: A Plan for Rebuilding Canada's Military* (Ottawa: Canadian Centre for Policy Alternatives, 2015), www.policyalternatives.ca/sites/default/files/uploads/ publications/National%20Office/2015/06/Smart_Defence.pdf.

5. Canada, Minister of National Defence, Advisory Committee on Administrative Efficiency, *Achieving Administrative Efficiency: Report to the Minister of National Defence*, August 21, 2003, iv.

6. Williams, *Reinventing Canadian Defence Procurement*, 75.

7. John Geddes, "How Was Ottawa to Choose Who Would Build Its Ships?" *Maclean's*, October 28, 2011.

8. Laura Payton, "Halifax, B.C. Yards Win Shipbuilding Work," *CBC News*, October 19, 2011, www.cbc.ca/news/politics/ halifax-b-c-yards-win-shipbuilding-work-1.1000979; Lee

Berthiaume, Robert Hiltz, and Marianne White, "East, West Coasts Win Shipbuilding Contracts, Québec Frozen Out," *Postmedia News*, October 19, 2011.

9. *Canada's Defence Industry: A Vital Partner Supporting Canada's Economic and National Interests* (Ottawa: Canadian Association of Defence and Security Industries, 2009).

10. See www.forces.gc.ca/en/business-how-to-do/irpda.page.

11. Jeffrey Simpson, "The Harper Government Loves the Military — in Theory," *Globe and Mail*, June 28, 2014.

12. Murray Brewster, "Federal Budget Sends Canadian Military's Equipment Buying Plan into Limbo; New Fighter Jets Likely off the Table," *National Post*, February 11, 2014.

13. For example, Charles Davies, "Canada's Defence Procurement Strategy: An End or a Beginning?" *Vimy Paper* 20 (September 2014).

14. Perry, "Four Steps for Fixing Canada's Trouble-Prone Procurement System" (see Introduction, n. 7).

15. J. Craig Stone, "Implementing the Defence Procurement Strategy: Is It Working?" *Policy Update*, Canadian Global Affairs Institute, July 2016.

16. Joyce Murray, "Real Change for Canada's Defence Policy," *Esprit de Corps* (August 2015), http://espritdecorps.ca/defence-platforms-liberal.

17. Terry Milewski, "Canada's Defence Budget Heads Back to the Future," *CBC News*, March 27, 2016, www.cbc.ca/news/politics/federal-budget-defence-milewski-1.3506670.

18. Cianfarani, "Three Steps Toward Better Defence Procurement" (see Introduction, n. 5).

5: FIXING DEFENCE PROCUREMENT IN CANADA

1. Kim Richard Nossal, Stéphane Roussel, and Stéphane Paquin, *The Politics of Canadian Foreign Policy*, 4th ed. (Montreal and Kingston: McGill-Queen's University Press, 2015), 27–29.

2. Nils Ørvik, "Defense Against Help: A Strategy for Small States," *Survival* 15, no. 5 (September/October 1973), 228–31.

3. Fisher, "Why the Super Hornets Will Force Canada out of Its Own North" (see chap. 2, n. 24).

4. David Pugliese, "Trudeau Sends Message to Military and DND Staff," *Ottawa Citizen*, November 13, 2015.

5. Canada, Department of National Defence, Chief of Force Development, *The Future Security Environment, 2013–2040* (Ottawa, 2014), http://publications.gc.ca/collections/collection_2015/mdn-dnd/D4-8-2-2014-eng.pdf.

6. Douglas G. Hartle, "Techniques and Processes of Administration," *Canadian Public Administration* 19, no. 1 (Spring 1976), 32.

7. On the 1987 process, see Norrin M. Ripsman, "Big Eyes and Empty Pockets: The Two Phrases of Conservative Defence Policy," and Nelson Michaud, "Bureaucratic Politics and the Making of the 1987 Defence White Paper," in Michaud and Nossal, eds., *Diplomatic Departures*, 100–12, 260–75.

8. Charles Davies, "Charting the Course Towards a New Canadian Defence Policy: Insights from Other Nations," *CDA Institute Analysis* (March 2016), www.cdainstitute.ca/images/Analysis/Davies_Analysis_March_2016.pdf.

9. "People are unlikely to participate in strategic reviews that result in merely an affirmation of the status quo, since that would suggest that the process was unnecessary — and so, too, their participation in it." David M. Edelstein and Ronald R. Krebs, "Delusions of Grand Strategy: The Problem with Washington's Planning Obsession," *Foreign Affairs* 94, no. 6 (November/December 2015), 114.

10. Alan Siaroff, "Two-and-a-Half-Party Systems and the Comparative Role of the 'Half,'" *Party Politics* 9, no. 3 (May 2003), 267–90.

11. Kim Richard Nossal, "Opening up the Policy Process: Does Party Make a Difference?" in Michaud and Nossal, eds., *Diplomatic Departures*, 276–89.

12. In January 2014, when he was still in opposition, Justin
    Trudeau expelled all senators from the Liberal parliamentary
    caucus as part of his efforts to reform the upper house. Those
    senators who were appointed to the Senate as Liberals refer to
    themselves as "Senate Liberals."

An index is available on the author's website for those readers who
would find it useful: https://nossalk.org/my-books/charlie-foxtrot.